RACE AND PARTY COMPETITION
IN BRITAIN

Race and Party Competition in Britain

Anthony M. Messina

CLARENDON PRESS
1989

Oxford University Press, Walton Street, Oxford OX2 6DP
Oxford New York Toronto
Delhi Bombay Calcutta Madras Karachi
Petaling Jaya Singapore Hong Kong Tokyo
Nairobi Dar es Salaam Cape Town
Melbourne Auckland
and associated companies in
Berlin Ibadan

Oxford is a trade mark of Oxford University Press

Published in the United States
by Oxford University Press, New York

British Library Cataloguing in Publication Data

Messina, Anthony M.
Race and party competition in Britain
1. Great Britain. Race relations. Policies,
1958–1988 of political parties
I. Title
305.8'00941
ISBN 0–19–827534–X

Library of Congress Cataloging in Publication Data
Messina, Anthony M.
Race and party competition in Britain/Anthony M. Messina   p.   cm.
Bibliography: p. Includes index.
1. Race relations—Political aspects—Great Britian.   2. Great
Britain—Politics and government—1945—   3. Racism–Political
aspects—Great Britain.   4. Political parties—Great Britain.
I. Title.
DA125.A1M47   1989   320.5'6'0941—dc19   89–30047
ISBN 0–19–827534–X

Typeset by Pentacor Ltd., High Wycombe, Bucks
Printed and bound in
Great Britain by Bookcraft Ltd,
Midsomer Norton, Bath

To my mother,
who influenced me to care passionately
and to the memory of my father,
who taught me to respect virtue

Parliamentary democracy and the party system have in recent years been criticized not only for their inability to solve some of our problems but also for their failure to reflect others adequately. It is not only some members of the public who are disenchanted. There are people inside active politics ... who believe that the alienation of Parliament from the people constitutes a genuine cause for concern. Political debates concentrating on economic and other management issues between government and opposition (whether Labour or Conservative) sometimes appear to blank out everything else, while a number of issues are not sufficiently discussed because they have not been fitted into the current pattern of political debate.

Tony Benn, *Arguments for Socialism*

The politician in the end is a voice and the political parties a chorus of voices. We hope that what we speak may be what others have been thinking and are ready to hear so that we may be a chord which will reverberate.

Enoch Powell, from *Enoch Powell and the Powellites*

Preface

Few topics in the post-war period have evoked as much passion among Britons, raised such important questions about the current and future condition of British society, and been as neglected by political scientists as the broad issue of race. In regard to this last point, John Solomos has observed that 'compared to studies of other aspects of British society, the political analysis of racism is relatively backward. There have been few studies of the politics of racism, and they compare very badly with the numerous sociological studies of race relations and anthropological studies of specific minority communities over the last two decades.'[1] British sociological scholarship on race, indeed, has become a small cottage industry, with dozens of book titles and articles added to the literature annually.[2] Yet the subject of race has been virtually ignored by both conventional and radical political science. Over the past thirty years only one or two major texts on the politics of race in Britain have been published each decade, and of these only two have linked race to other public policy issues or areas of governmental responsibility.[3]

Unlike much previous scholarship, this study focuses not on the social origins or historical roots of racism or racial conflict in Britain, but on the political dimensions of race, and specifically the dilemmas this area of public policy has raised for the Conservative and Labour parties since the late 1950s. Race has not been adequately considered in this context. Paul Foot's *Immigration and Race in British Politics*, and his 1969

[1] John Solomos, 'Trends in the Political Analysis of Racism', *Political Studies*, 34.2, June 1986, 313.

[2] See e.g. Sheila Patterson, *Dark Strangers*, Bloomington, Indiana Univ. Press, 1964; John Rex and Robert Moore, *Race, Community, and Conflict*, London, IRR/OUP, 1967; Daniel Lawrence, *Black Migrants, White Natives*, London, CUP, 1974; Catherine Jones, *Immigration and Social Policy in Britain*, London, Tavistock, 1977; John Rex and Sally Tomlison, *Coloured Immigrants in a British City*, London, Routledge, 1979; and Muhammad Anwar, *The Myth of Return*, London, Heinemann, 1979.

[3] See Ira Katznelson, *Black Men, White Cities*, London, OUP, 1973; and Gary P. Freeman, *Immigrant Labor and Racial Conflict in Industrial Societies*, Princeton, Princeton Univ. Press, 1979.

polemic, *The Rise of Enoch Powell*, for example, offer early evidence of the difficulties the emergence of a multiracial society and race-related conflict in Britain created for the major political parties. But these books lack a theoretical framework and are now quite dated. The voluminous literature on non-white immigration patterns and settlement[4] and Layton-Henry's well-researched text on the politics of race in Britain provide much useful historical material.[5] However, these volumes conspicuously fail to link the politics of race to the broader political currents of which it is obviously a part.[6]

Perhaps the closest work to this book in its approach to the study of the post–1958 politics of race in Britain is Katznelson's *Black Men, White Cities*, which initially inspired me. Even the casual reader will not fail to notice that Katznelson's macro-analysis, and much of his micro-analysis, of the politics of race in Britain have been incorporated into and extended in this volume. Chapter 3, for example, re-examines the role which Community Relations Councils have played historically in depoliticizing race-related issues. Like Katznelson's book, this study locates the political conflict over race issues in Britain, and specifically non-white immigration, within a broader political context. However, unlike *Black Men, White Cities*, this study is not primarily concerned with how non-whites have been incorporated into British political life— although Chapters 3 and 7 pay considerable attention to these questions—but rather with why and how the Conservative and Labour parties in the 1964–75 period attempted to keep race-related issues off the political agenda. Or, to put it more succinctly, this book attempts to explain why and how the major parties did not 'compete' on race. To a considerable extent *Black Men, White Cities* also considered these questions.

---

[4] See K. Jones and A. D. Smith, *The Economic Impact of Commonwealth Immigration*, Cambridge, CUP, 1970; Howard Palmer, *Immigration and the Rise of Multiculturalism*, London, Heinemann, 1970; Hugh Tinker, *The Banyan Tree*, New York, OUP, 1977; Anwar, op. cit.; and Freeman, op. cit.

[5] Zig Layton-Henry, *The Politics of Race in Britain*, London, Allen and Unwin, 1984. For a longer historical overview see Paul B. Rich, *Race and Empire in British Politics*, Cambridge, CUP, 1986.

[6] A stimulating, although ultimately unsatisfying, recent attempt to link the politics of race in Britain to broader political currents can be found in Jim Bulpitt, 'Continuity, Autonomy, and Peripheralization: The Autonomy of the Centre's Race Statecraft in England', in Z. Layton-Henry and P. B. Rich (eds.), *Race, Government and Politics in Britain*, London, Macmillan, 1986, pp. 17–44. See also Brian D. Jacobs, *Black Politics and Urban Crisis in Britain*, Cambridge, CUP, 1986.

However, as many of Katznelson's assumptions and arguments have been undermined by political events in the 1970s
and 1980s, alternative lines of inquiry and argument are now
appropriate.

Like most intellectual products, this study has had a long
gestation and has benefited from the assistance, time, and
generosity of many people. It initially grew out of a modest
research paper, written in 1979 at the Massachusetts Institute
of Technology, entitled 'Race, the Political Parties and Citizen
Groups: Depoliticization and Political Conflict in Britain'.
From research paper to Ph.D. dissertation the analysis was
extended and further refined in several conference papers,
which were subsequently published. A version of Chapter 3
appeared in *Ethnic and Racial Studies*. Chapter 4 draws heavily
from an article in *Political Studies*, and a condensed version of
Chapter 5 appeared in *The Review of Politics*. Chapter 6 updates
the information presented in a 1985 article published in
Parliamentary Affairs. I thank these journals for permission to
use the materials contained in these articles.

I also wish to express my gratitude to my dissertation
committee at MIT. Suzanne Berger, my dissertation super-
visor, was tremendously helpful and intellectually supportive.
Without her steady guidance, advice, and prodding this study
would not have been possible. Walter Dean Burnham offered
stimulating criticism and invaluable insights and suggestions.
His writing on political parties, elections, and non-élite
representation has forever influenced my thinking and the
scholarship of an entire generation of comparative political
scientists. Thomas Ferguson was a friend in countless ways. It
is a pity that his impressive insights into party coalition-
building in the United States have not been applied to the
United Kingdom.

Thanks are due to the many English local politicians,
Members of Parliament, librarians, political-party research-
ers, activists, community relations officers, and other busy
people who kindly gave of their time. Usha Prashar, former
Director of The Runnymede Trust, was particularly generous
with advice. Chapter 3 could not have been written without her
assistance. I wish also to thank those officials at the Commission
for Racial Equality and the Conservative and Labour party
headquarters whom I interviewed. Peter Alexander of the

Socialist Workers' Party in Ealing borough was an especially friendly and co-operative subject.

Don Studlar and Zig Layton-Henry provided some of the key data which allowed me to complete Chapter 7 and, of course, their respected scholarship on the politics of race in Britain is cited liberally throughout this study. While my analysis of post–1958 developments in this policy area differs somewhat from their previous interpretations, it has been both informed and stimulated by them.

A considerable debt is owed to Harvard University's Center for European Studies which provided funds for the initial exploratory research, and the National Science Foundation whose timely grant ensured that the early manuscript would be completed. Support from a Jesse H. Jones Faculty Research Grant at the University of Notre Dame permitted me to collect many of the materials which inform Chapter 7.

I am deeply grateful to Betty and John Low for housing me in London, offering companionship, and patiently answering all my simple and sometimes silly American questions. Alexander, David, and Katie Low provided endless and necessary distractions during my field research.

A special and permanent debt is owed to my friend, colleague, analyst, coach, editor, and wife Frances Hagopian, without whom this study could not have been initiated and completed. Only she knows how necessary were her criticisms, care, and intellectual contributions. I only wish I could satisfy her standards.

Finally, I wish to thank Ira Katznelson, whom I hope to meet one day. Over the years I have heard and read many criticisms of *Black Men, White Cities*, but I have yet to discover a more penetrating analysis of the early politics of race in Britain. *Black Men, White Cities*, indeed, not only occupies a unique place in the literature on race in Britain, but it remains, fifteen years after it was first published, a seminal work in the general literature on post-war British politics. In a very real sense *Black Men, White Cities* first illuminated the intellectual dark cave in which the author and other contemporary students of the politics of race in Britain continue to grope.

A.M.M.

Contents

Figures and Maps

List of Tables

I

Introduction

Race relations and state policies which regulate the immigration of non-whites into Britain have persisted since the late 1950s as socially divisive and politically charged issues which have challenged the capacity of the political system, and especially the major political parties, to respond.[1] Few would deny the salience of race in post-war British society and politics. Since the arrival of the first large group of New Commonwealth immigrants in Britain in the late 1940s, periodic racial disturbances have flared, a racist, neo-Fascist movement has surged and declined, and successive governments, in response to illiberal popular sentiment, have radically altered the country's immigration and nationality statutes. A 'hidden mover of votes', race is believed by many to have influenced the outcome of at least two general elections in the 1970s and contributed to partisan dealignment.[2] Most social scientists concur that pervasive conditions of racism and non-white disadvantage and alienation were prime causes of England's urban riots of the early and mid-1980s; some of the worst violence seen in Britain in recent history.[3] Moreover, contrary to the perception of some observers that race was not a factor in the 1987 general election, racism continued to penetrate the politics of local

[1] For a general overview of the politics of race in Britain see Zig Layton-Henry, *The Politics of Race in Britain*, London, Allen and Unwin, 1984. Also see Paul Foot, *Immigration and Race in British Politics*, Harmondsworth, Penguin, 1965.

[2] Ivor Crewe, 'How to Win a Landslide without Really Trying: Why the Conservatives Won in 1983', in, Austin Ranney (ed.), *Britain at the Polls 1983*, Durham, NC, AEI/Duke Univ. Press, 1985, p. 173. See Layton-Henry, op. cit., pp. 57–80; *Participation of Ethnic Minorities in the General Election October 1974*, London, Community Relations Commission, 1975; Douglas E. Schoen, *Enoch Powell and the Powellites*, New York, St. Martin's, 1977, p. 276; and Paul Whiteley, 'The Decline of Partisan Allegiance in Britain and the National Front Vote', unpublished paper, 1978.

[3] See Ceri Peach, 'A Geographical Perspective on the 1981 Urban Riots in England', *Ethnic and Racial Studies*, 9.3, July 1986, 396–411; and John Benyon (ed.), *Scarman and After*, New York, Pergamon, 1984.

constituencies and racial tensions to disturb the Labour party's internal affairs.[4] Yet, despite the persistent salience of race in British politics and society, open and frank political discussion of race-related public policy has been rare. Until relatively recently, race-related issues were conspicuously absent from the national political agenda in Britain.[5]

The absence of race from the political agenda, while perplexing in itself, is perhaps even more puzzling given the considerable evidence which points to the deliberate neglect of race-related issues by the major political parties.[6] Rather than elevating citizen concerns on race to the political agenda, as democratic theory would have predicted in circumstances of electorally competitive two-partism, the Conservative and Labour parties pursued multiple strategies to exclude race-related issues from inter-party debate and public, political discussion. On its narrowest and most modest level, this book attempts to explain the obvious motivations of the major political parties, the methods they employed to keep race-related issues off the political agenda, and the ultimate consequences of their actions. More broadly and ambitiously, this study locates the post–1958 national and local politics of race within the larger context of what Gamble has coined the 'politics of support', the Conservative and Labour parties' intense contest for votes and political office in the post-war period.[7] The overarching argument presented here is that the post–1958 politics of race in Britain have been inextricably linked to the requirements of and the patterns of inter-party interaction engendered by the Conservative and Labour parties' post-war political consensus. The most significant consequences of this link were the formation of a bipartisan racial consensus and the suspension of political party competition on race-related issues between 1964 and 1975.

That race should be neglected by Britain's major political parties is perhaps not surprising. Since 1945 political élites have been preoccupied with Britain's economic difficulties;

---

[4] See e.g. Steve Platt, 'Spoiling for a Fight', *New Society*, 29 May 1987, 20–3; and Sarah Benton, 'A Watershed for Black Politics', *New Statesman*, 24 Apr. 1987, 12–13.

[5] See Donley T. Studlar, ' "Waiting for the Catastrophe": Race and the Political Agenda in Britain', *Patterns of Prejudice*, 19.1, Jan. 1985, 3–15.

[6] See Layton-Henry, op. cit.

[7] Andrew Gamble, *The Conservative Nation*, London, Routledge, 1974.

understandably given the country's post-war economic decline. However, while economic problems have dominated political élite discourse, non-élites have often been concerned with other matters. Indeed, the persistent popularity of the political gadflies Tony Benn and Enoch Powell attests to their acute sensitivity and responsiveness to what might be described as the neglected public agenda.[8]

Until very recently, few scholars would have entertained even the possibility of a neglected public agenda in the British context. Unprepared to discover serious flaws in Britain's seemingly exemplary political arrangements, social scientists overlooked evidence of political disillusionment among citizens and a divergence between political élite agendas and voters' concerns.[9] However, by the 1970s, numerous political tremors converged with concrete evidence of partisan dealignment to shake traditional perceptions. In particular, the long-held supposition that intense, party competition facilitates the identification of and solution to salient public problems became increasingly questioned. To more than a few observers, Britain's competitive electoral arrangements suddenly appeared to be disfunctional to responsible and representative government.[10] Far from helping to illuminate and frame the public agenda, intense two-party competition obscured it, it was claimed.

Recent doubts about the merits of British party competition, especially in circumstances of two-partism,[11] raise two

[8] The public aggenda may be defined as a set of 'issues which have achieved public interest and visibility, and which a sizeable proportion of the public consider are significant and merit action. It is likely to be broader and more general than comparable institutional agendas, and distinguishable communities and groups (different "publics") may have dissimilar agendas'. John Benyon, 'Going Through the Motions: The Political Agenda, the 1981 Riots and the Scarman Inquiry', *Parliamentary Affairs*, 38.4, Autumn 1985, 411.

[9] See e.g. Donley T. Studlar and Susan Welch, 'Mass Attitudes on Political Issues in Britain', *Comparative Political Studies*, 14.3, Oct. 1981, 327–55; and Schoen, op. cit., pp. 201–2.

[10] See S. E. Finer, *The Changing British Party System 1945–79*, Washington, DC, American Enterprise Institute, 1980.

[11] According to Giovanni Sartori, the 'lenient conditions for a system that functions according to the rules of two-partism are: (i) two parties are in a position to compete for an absolute majority of seats; (ii) one of the two parties actually succeeds in winning a sufficient parliamentary majority; (iii) this party is willing to govern alone; (iv) alternation or rotation in power remains a credible expectation.' *Parties and Party Systems*, Cambridge, CUP, 1977.

related questions: what is implied by party competition; and what is the link, if any, between party competition and the public agenda? Although we can only address ourselves to these questions briefly, both are relevant to our investigation of the national and local post–1958 politics of race. A central assumption of this book is that few significant public-policy areas can be fruitfully studied, or the larger post–1945 course of public affairs in Britain adequately comprehended, without reference to the post-war political competition of the Conservative and Labour parties. Moreover, as students of politics from Schumpeter to Key have astutely observed, party competition is the linchpin of democratic politics.

PERCEPTIONS OF PARTY COMPETITION

For political theorists such as Downs, Schumpeter, and others, democratic politics begins, and to a considerable degree ends, with the electoral struggle between political parties.[12] According to Downs, 'a *democratic* government is one chosen periodically by means of popular elections in which two or more political parties compete for the votes of all adults'.[13] For Schumpeter, 'the democratic method is that institutional arrangement for arriving at political decisions in which individuals acquire the power to decide by means of a competition for the people's vote'.[14] Central to both authors' conception of democracy is the opportunity for voters to select freely a team of party leaders who define, through their policies, the public good. However, it is quite clear from their analyses that there is no expectation that politically competitive parties must offer distinct programmes or policy courses.[15]

[12] A thoughtful discussion of this issue is contained in Karen L. Remmer, *Party Competition in Argentina and Chile*, Lincoln, NE, Univ. of Nebraska Press, 1984.
[13] Anthony Downs, *An Economic Theory of Democracy*, New York, Harper and Row, 1957, p. 34.
[14] Joseph A. Schumpeter, *Capitalism, Socialism, and Democracy*, New York, Harper and Row, 1975, p. 269.
[15] Both authors more or less assume that in competing for votes parties will adopt policies that, when implemented, will serve the public interest. This view is also prevalent in R. T. McKenzie, *British Political Parties*, London, Praeger, 1963.

In the British context, it has often been observed that the post-war years were a period of fervid political-party competition. According to Beer:

The competition of these two parties, exacerbated by their near even electoral strength, was intense. The normative premises of the collectivist polity, moreover, by lifting the restraints on government responsibility of the precollectivist liberal state, legitimated a much greater scope for expansive competition.[16]

That government assumed greater responsibilities after 1945, especially in economic affairs, is indisputable. However, to what degree did the growth of government or the near equal representation of the parties in Parliament in the 1950s and 1960s precipitate intense, party competition?

If, as Schumpeter and others have implied, the essence of party competition is the struggle for elective office, then British inter-party relations in the fifties and sixties were extremely competitive. The inordinate length and detail of the general-election manifestos of the major parties, their use of survey data and market advertising to tailor electoral appeals to particular voting blocs, and the obsession and considerable financial investment of the parties in electorally marginal parliamentary constituencies between 1950 and 1974 all support Beer's contention that party competition was intense.[17] To highlight, for example, the efforts of the parties in regard to the manifesto: before 1945 general-election manifestos were primarily vague statements of the programmatic orientation of the parties. Rose has noted that 'at the turn of the century, party manifestos were brief exhortations to voters, not detailed programmes. In 1900, the Conservatives won office with a manifesto that made only two general commitments: to maintain the Imperial Power in South Africa, and to strengthen the nation's military force.'[18] Even as late as 1935, in the midst of world crisis, Labour's general-election manifesto was only a few pages in length. However, by 1959 the manifesto as a promissory document had become

[16] Samuel H. Beer, *Britain Against Itself*, New York, Norton, 1982, pp. 16–17.
[17] For a discussion of e.g. the Conservative party's 'critical seats' exercise during the 1970 general election, see David Butler and Michael Pinto-Duschinsky, *The British General Election of 1970*, New York, St. Martin's, 1971, pp. 288–91.
[18] Richard Rose, *Do Parties Make a Difference?*, London, Macmillan, 1980, p. 54.

increasingly important. In order to attract the broadest possible electoral support, the election programmes of the parties became extremely detailed, more than doubling in average length from the pre-war 1922–35 period to the later period between 1945 and 1959. In an escalation of manifesto madness the Conservative Central Office boasted in 1974 that of the 105 pledges contained in the 1970 Tory general-election manifesto, the Heath government, in less than four years, had implemented 97. Rose has noted that Labour party head-quarters claimed in 1979 that within the previous five years it had produced '70 "major" NEC statements, a 60,000-word 1976 programme and commissioned more than 2000 research papers'.[19]

Political party activity aimed at gaining office was indeed frenetic after 1950, spurred by the near-equal electoral strength of the parties and their scramble to court politically uncommitted voters. Nevertheless, we might ask: how did the electoral struggle of the major parties affect the substance of their policies? If by party competition we understand, as many British politics textbooks over the years have implied, that alternative teams of leaders offer divergent or 'competing' policy courses, then British party politics were highly uncom-petitive for most of the post-war period. If anything, the frenetic electoral struggle between the major parties fostered inter-party consensus in many areas of public policy. Below we shall briefly examine two facets of consensual politics: the convergence of party policies; and the withdrawal by the Conservative and Labour parties of a number of salient issues from the electoral arena. From this discussion we will proceed to a succinct, minimalist definition of political party competition.

PARTY POLITICS IN THE BUTSKELLITE ERA

(i) Consensual elections and policies

The essential elements of the Conservative and Labour parties' post-war political consensus are well known and have

[19] Rose, *Do Parties Make a Difference?*, p. 56.

been the focus of considerable scholarship.[20] Coined from the names of the prominent Tory progressive R. A. Butler and the Labour leader Hugh Gaitskell, the term 'Butskellism' described the comprehensive agreement of the Conservative and Labour parties on most economic, political, and social questions. Punnett has observed that 'after the ideological debates that took place during the 1945–51 period . . . the long period of Conservative rule between 1951 and 1964 and the 1964–70 period of Labour Government, produced merely conflict over details'.[21] Although perhaps overstated, this conclusion reflected a certain reality: during the 1950s and 1960s the parties pursued a remarkably similar course. From a mutual commitment to NATO and a nuclear-based defence, through their Keynesian management of a 'mixed' economy, to the creation and maintenance of a welfare state, the major parties' post-war consensus defined the parameters within which public policy was conceived and implemented for almost three decades.

Less well known, but at least as noteworthy as evidence of consensus politics, were the similar platforms adopted by the major parties during general-election campaigns. Robertson's analysis of the election manifestos of the Conservative and Labour parties between 1924 and 1966, for example, reveals that their positions on most major political and economic issues converged in the 1950s.[22] By 1964 the major parties shared similar economic policies and goals, with their manifesto positions converging toward the centre of Robertson's scale (see Figure 1). Of particular interest is that the distance between the policies of the parties after 1945 was considerably less than between 1929 and 1935. Indeed, the distance between the economic goals and policies of the major parties in 1964 was only one-fifth as wide as in 1931; in 1966 it was still less than a third. Moreover, even when the policies of the parties were not converging they exhibited a certain harmony. Between 1945 and 1966 the shift in ideological

---

[20] See, e.g. Samuel H. Beer, *British Politics in the Collectivist Age*, New York, Vintage, 1966, pp. 352–9; and R. M. Punnett, *British Government and Politics*, New York, Norton, 1971, pp. 22–8.

[21] Punnett, op. cit., p. 24.

[22] David Robertson, *A Theory of Party Competition*, London, Wiley, 1976, pp. 97–136.

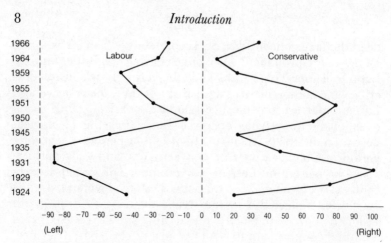

1966
1964   Labour   Conservative
1959
1955
1951
1950
1945
1935
1931
1929
1924

-90 -80 -70 -60 -50 -40 -30 -20 -10 0 10 20 30 40 50 60 70 80 90 100
(Left)   (Right)

FIG. I. Distance between major-party manifestos on major economic
issues, 1924–1966 (*Source*: D. Robertson, *A Theory of Party Competition*,
London, Wiley, 1976, p. 98.

direction (left or right) from the previous election of each
party's policies was harmonious in four of six campaigns.

Robertson's study and more impressionistic accounts of the
convergence of the parties would, of course, be less powerful if
party rhetoric had created an illusion of 'choice', that is, if the
electorate had perceived that there were meaningful differences between the parties, despite the evidence to the
contrary. Miller, for instance, has persuasively argued that a
party's position is probably best defined 'by looking at the
receiving, rather than the sending, end of the campaign
communications process'.[23]

Yet, even when voters' perceptions are considered, the
evidence still supports the thesis that the parties' policies
converged. Indeed, Table 1.1 yields two interesting insights.
First, as the post-war period progressed, an increasing
number of citizens became aware of an operating bipartisan
political consensus. Between 1948 and 1958 the percentage of
citizens seeing the parties as 'all much of a muchness' more
than doubled; by the 1970s more than two in five citizens
consistently expressed the opinion that there were no significant differences between the parties. Second, trends in public

[23] W. L. Miller, 'What Was the Profit in Following the Crowd? The Effectiveness
of Party Strategies on Immigration and Devolution', *British Journal of Political Science*,
10.1, Jan. 1980, 20.

opinion on party differences paralleled, with a predictable time lag, the rise and fall of the parties' political consensus. It is no coincidence that the 1983 and 1987 poll results on party differences more closely resemble those of the 1950s than the 1970s. By 1983 the public policy orientation of the major

TABLE 1.1 *Public perceptions of inter-party differences, 1948–1987*
(% of respondents)

(1) *Do you think it makes a great deal of difference which political party runs your country?*

	Yes	No	Don't know
1948	70	20	10
1949	72	21	7

(2) *Do you think that there is any really important difference between the parties, or are they all much of a muchness?*

	Are important differences	Much of a muchness	Don't know
1951	71	20	9
1952	59	32	9
1954	53	39	8
1955	74	20	6
1958	40	46	14
1959	66	29	5
1961	54	36	10
1962	45	47	8
1963	49	39	12
1964	59	32	9
1965	56	31	13
1966	55	37	8
1970	54	41	5
1972	47	48	5
1974	54	41	5
1977	34	60	6
1979	54	41	5
1983	67	28	5
1987	74	24	2

(3) 1966: *Would you say there is as much difference between the two main parties as there used to be?*

	All	Conservative	Labour	Liberal
Yes	35	35	39	23
No	50	50	47	65
Don't know	15	15	14	12

Sources: The Gallup International Public Opinion Polls, Great Britain, 1937–75, New York, Random House, 1976; Richard Rose, *Do Parties Make a Difference?,* London, Macmillan, 1980, Table 3.5; *Gallup Political Index,* 1983–7, London, Social Surveys (Gallup Poll) Ltd.; National Opinion Polls Ltd., 1966.

parties had diverged—by then their political consensus had eroded—and these differences did not escape the notice of the British electorate. Hence, whether the content of the parties' electoral platforms or voters' perceptions of party differences are examined, the evidence supports the existence of a bipartisan political consensus during most of the post-war period. During this time the major parties offered British voters more of an 'echo' than a 'choice'.

(ii) Conspiracies of silence

A second manifestation of political consensus after 1950 was the tacit agreement of the Conservative and Labour parties to exclude certain issues from the national political agenda. In Chapter 2 we shall identify the principal strategies the major parties employed to depoliticize race-related issues. However, race was hardly the only issue the parties avoided in the post-war period; Scottish devolution, the nuclear question, Ulster, and British relations with the European Economic Community were also generally absent from election manifestos, political speeches, and parliamentary debates.[24]

How salient were and are these issues to British voters? The unavailability of consistent and penetrating longitudinal

[24] See e.g. Butler and Pinto-Duschinsky, op. cit., p. 159; Peter Malone, *The British Nuclear Deterrent,* New York, St. Martin's, 1984, pp. 26–44; and Bruce E. Cain, 'Trends in British Politics', Working Paper, California Institute of Technology, 171, Aug. 1977.

survey data makes it difficult to be certain.[25] Nevertheless, two things can be said with some confidence. First, most of these issues were or have been salient for a considerable period. The multidimensional race problem, for instance, was among the most visible and politically charged areas of public policy in the 1960s and 1970s; during this period over 80 per cent of the electorate felt that too many immigrants had been admitted into Britain and in 1968 more than 25 per cent identified 'immigrants' as the most urgent problem facing the country (see Table 1.2). Through the early 1980s more than four out of five citizens saw controlling immigration as a high priority and almost 50 per cent consistently felt the government wasn't saying enough about the issue.[26] Similarly, in the late 1950s and early 1960s the interrelated policy areas of defence, disarmament, and nuclear weapons ranked at the top of citizen concerns. Indeed, at one point in 1959 the public considered the hydrogen bomb/disarmament controversy as the most urgent problem confronting the government.[27]

Second, the political significance of these issues, and especially their influence on the perceptions of parties by the voters, have probably been underestimated. Unlike equally or more salient economic issues, which the electorate has often viewed as beyond the competence or control of the parties, other problems, for example non-white immigration, race relations, nuclear disarmament, and EEC membership, have been perceived by the public as politically manageable and the responsibility of parties and government.[28] Hence, it is possible that the neglect of these issues by the major parties

[25] Over the years Gallup has regularly asked the public to identify the 'most urgent' problem facing the government and the 'most important' problem facing the country. Apart from the fact that these questions only indirectly measure issue saliency, the responses to them have often been collected under categories which differ from one poll to the next.

[26] *Gallup Political Index*, 1978–82, London, Social Surveys (Gallup Poll) Limited.

[27] In August 1959 the nuclear disarmament issue ranked higher than unemployment and the overall economic situation. If combined with the category of foreign affairs/war it was cited as the most urgent problem by 39% of respondents.

[28] In a Gallup poll conducted in March 1978 63% of respondents disagreed with the statement that 'little can be done' about reducing immigration. George H. Gallup (ed.), *The International Gallup Polls, Public Opinion 1978*, Wilmington, DE, Scholarly Resources Inc., 1980. For evidence that the British public ceased to expect the major parties to solve Britain's post–1950s economic difficulties, see James E. Alt, *The Politics of Economic Decline*, Cambridge, CUP, 1979.

TABLE 1.2. *Public opinion on immigration and race relations, 1963–1986*
(% of respondents)

(1) Do you think too many immigrants have been let into this country or not?

	1963	1964	1966	1969	1970
(a) Yes	83	81	81	87	85
(b) No	12	13	14	10	10
(c) Don't know	5	6	5	3	5

How strongly do you feel about this?

	1964	1966	1969	1970
(a) Very strongly	52	54	56	50
(b) Fairly strongly	34	33	30	34
(c) Not very strongly	14	13	14	16

(2) What do you say is the most urgent problem facing the country at the present time?

	1968	1970	1972
(a) Economic affairs	52	55	56
(b) Immigrants	27	10	12
(c) International affairs	10	6	13
(d) Labour relations	7	13	10
(e) Defence	3	2	0
(f) Other	1	14	9

(3) How important would you say controlling immigration is at the moment?*

	1978	1979	1980	1981	1982
(a) Extremely	66	58	59	59	59
(b) Quite	25	30	24	24	25
(c) Not very	4	5	9	9	10
(d) Not at all	2	3	4	4	3
(e) Don't know	2	5	4	4	3

(4) *How important would you say improving race relations is at the moment?**

		1978	1979	1980	1981	1982
(a)	Extremely	33	34	38	47	46
(b)	Quite	40	39	41	35	40
(c)	Not very	15	16	12	11	8
(d)	Not at all	5	4	4	3	4
(e)	Don't know	7	6	5	4	3

(5) *Do you think . . . (immigrants, coloured persons) . . . are very serious social problems today?*

	1976	1979	1982	1983	1984	1985	1986
Agree	70	48	45	39	32	34	38

* Gallup no longer asks this question.

Sources: David Butler and Donald Stokes, *Political Change in Britain*, 2nd edn., New York, St. Martin's, 1974, p. 461; *The Gallup International Public Opinion Polls Great Britain, 1937–75,* New York, Random House, 1976; *Gallup Political Index* 1976–86, London, Social Surveys (Gallup Poll) Ltd.

eroded partisan attachments. At the very least, the reluctance of the Conservative and Labour parties to deal with these issues must have undermined citizen confidence in them.

Why then did the major parties avoid these issues? Most have seriously divided the parties internally and/or threatened to disturb that fraction of the electorate, the so-called 'swing' or 'floating' voters, whom party leaders believed decided general election outcomes.[29] Such voters were seen as important because of the small electoral swings at general elections in the 1950s and 1960s, and the near-equal representation of the parties in Parliament. As Gamble explains the calculations of party leaders:

The [new] consensus . . . led to a declining interest in 'ideology' and a growing interest in 'rational' electioneering in both parties. It became plausible to suppose that the consensus between the parties on the state reflected a consensus in the nation. In the spectrum of political opinion from right to left, the majority of the electors had

[29] See Andrew Gamble, op. cit., pp. 65–70.

moved towards the middle, the breeding ground of the floaters, leaving only minorities clustered at the extremes.

Such a notion was clearly fiction, but it was an important fiction. For it suggested a particular electoral strategy. Success in the political market now seemed to depend on capturing the centre and winning the support of the floaters.[30]

Subscribing to the Downsian premiss that these voters were 'centre-inclined', political 'moderates', Conservative and Labour leaders sought to depoliticize issues which could undermine their centrist image and destabilize their broader political consensus.[31] The absence of a political middle ground on many of these issues and their characteristic cross-cutting of traditional party lines meant they could only be neutralized politically if both major parties withdrew them from the electoral market-place.

The convergence of Conservative and Labour policy on race and other cross-cutting issues was not, of course, exceptional. As Miller argues:

It is not in the least surprising that . . . it should happen frequently. With only two parties and a multitude of issues they cannot be expected to disagree about everything. On those issues that were originally central to their existence they may continue to disagree, but British parties are not dissolved and recreated as rapidly as new issues come and go. So new issues are likely to cross-cut old party divisions. Even if parties could be broken and reconstituted along new lines for each election . . . the basic problem remains as long as two cross-cutting issues coexist. A two-party system must treat one issue as the basis for political division and the other as a dangerously misleading distraction that would erode party discipline if not suppressed.[32]

While not entirely incorrect, Miller's argument is nevertheless misleading. First, race was not just any cross-cutting issue in the sixties and seventies. Rather, as the then Cabinet Minister Richard Crossman noted in his diary entry of 2 August 1965, 'Politically, fear of immigration is the most powerful undertow today.'[33] Cain estimates that in 1966

---

[30] Andrew Gamble, op. cit., p. 67.
[31] Ibid., p. 101.
[32] Miller, op. cit., pp. 16–17.
[33] Richard Crossman, *The Diaries of a Cabinet Minister Volume I, 1964–66*, New York, Holt, Rinehart and Winston, 1975, p. 299.

sentiment within the electorate that there were too many immigrants in Britain was virtually universal.[34] As party leaders were well aware, an initiative to neutralize race as an electoral issue was required because of the passions it stirred among party activists and a significant percentage of the electorate. Moreover, the major parties did not consider questions of race, nuclear weapons, Britain's membership of the Common Market, and Scottish devolution so differently from other issues. Indeed, while the politics of Butskellism prevailed, major questions of public policy were excluded from political debate, leaving 'the parties with disagreements over minor aspects of policy'.[35] Nurtured and defended by a generation of post-war party leaders, the Conservative and Labour parties' political consensus encouraged a bipartisan approach to public policy bordering on collusion. For over two decades political conflict over public policy was more visible within than between the major parties.[36]

The pervasiveness and comprehensiveness of the post-war political consensus and its influence in fostering a convergence of major-party policies and the exclusion of relevant public-policy issues from the electoral arena are problematic for the view that party relations during most of the post-war period were intensely competitive. At the very least, these developments cast doubt on the usefulness of defining party competition primarily as the struggle among parties to gain elective office. As noted above, not all students of contemporary party politics would agree. Robertson, for example, argues that 'party competition is about the selection of governments first and secondarily, if at all, about the representation of anyone'.[37] However, the tendency of political parties in liberal democracies to pursue consensual policy courses, and in particular the propensity of post-war British parties to neglect issues salient to millions of voters, should not be confused with a theory or definition of party competition. Above all, inter-party collusive behaviour, whether explicit or implicit, dimin-

[34] Cain, op. cit.
[35] Punnett, op. cit., p. 24.
[36] Dennis Kavanagh, 'Whatever Happened to Consensus Politics?', *Political Studies*, 33.4, Dec. 1985, 529–46.
[37] Robertson, op. cit., p. 14.

ishes the potential for and is incompatible with party
competitive politics.

In addition to its electoral dimension, competition among
political parties implies five things in a liberal democracy:
parties offer concrete policies in addition to alternative teams
of leaders; these policies can be and are comprehended by a
substantial percentage of the electorate; a majority of voters
find the policies of more than one party relevant; parties
publicly speak to, rather than past, one another on most
public-policy issues; and most salient citizen concerns which
can be addressed politically are addressed by at least one
political party.[38] These conditions are never fully apparent, of
course, even in the most politically competitive circumstances.
If only because of the constraints associated with the
prevailing 'politics of power', all major parties of government
are under constant pressure to adopt consensual electoral
programmes and to avoid policy commitments which might
conflict with the anticipated 'responsibilities' of office.[39] Yet,
the improbable, simultaneous satisfaction of these conditions
does not diminish our argument that they are integral to party
competition. Indeed, these conditions only partly define it.
Even their perfect realization does not signal ideal or perfect
party competition.

These conditions are merely minimal standards by which
parties can be judged to be acting competitively. In this
respect, they exact very little from parties and party behaviour. It is not necessarily implied, for instance, that parties
offer policy positions in good faith. Moreover, once in office,
parties need not succeed in implementing their electoral
programmes. What is implied is that parties, and specifically
party leaders, do not collude to make elections simply a
conflict of personalities or images, and that inter-party

---

[38] It seems reasonable that, in the absence of these conditions, elections may
remove leaders, but not necessarily policies, and that voters cannot choose rationally
between sets of party leaders. Robertson, op. cit., p. 21.

[39] Gamble, op. cit.

dialogue reflects the central legitimate political concerns of the electorate. Indeed, in open, plural societies major parties can hardly avoid satisfying these conditions, except when they collude not to do so. In a liberal democracy lively inter-party debate and partisan conflict over public policy naturally follow from party competition, whereas inter-party policy consensus and the exclusion of major issues from the political agenda signal its partial suspension.[40]

The incompatibility of inter-party policy consensus with party-competitive politics is underscored by the increased significance of intra-party politics once party policies converge. When artificial consensus prevails between the parties, conflict and competition within each party inevitably escalate, as anti-consensus forces concentrate their attention on internal party affairs. The replacement of inter-party competition with intra-party conflict has far-reaching and mostly negative consequences,[41] not the least of which is the transference of meaningful policy debate from the electoral arena to party committee rooms and annual party conferences. Party activists in these circumstances can often enjoy greater political voice than the general electorate. Yet, even then, party leaders will not necessarily respond to the policy preferences of their rank and file. Given the hierarchical structures and authoritarian practices of most political parties, and particularly British parties, party leaders can normally insulate themselves and their policies from grass roots pressures.[42] Consequently, inter-party consensus, once concluded among party leaders, is likely to endure for a considerable period, even in the face of stiff opposition. At this point, the democratic and representational advantages of Key's 'organized' politics are almost completely lost.[43] 'In' and 'out' parties remain easy to identify, but alternation in office between the two will have little impact on the course of public policy.

Our investigation of the post–1958 politics of race in Britain challenges at least two conventional assumptions about the

[40] See A. M. Gamble and S. A. Walkland, *The British Party System and Economic Policy 1945–83*, Oxford, OUP, 1984, pp. 38–9.

[41] See Sartori, op. cit., pp. 49–50.

[42] See McKenzie, op. cit.

[43] V. O. Key Jr., *Southern Politics in State and Nation*, Knoxville, TN, Univ. of Tennessee Press, 1984, pp. 298–310.

dynamics of party competition. First, it disputes the Downsian supposition that in a two-party system both parties
nearly always adopt any course that a majority of the
electorate strongly favour, 'no matter what strategies the
parties are following'.[44] As we shall see in Chapters 2 and 5,
most voters clearly preferred that the major parties pay
greater attention to race-related issues. Yet, between 1964 and
1975 Conservative and Labour leaders adopted explicit
measures to extricate race issues from the political agenda.
Second, this study challenges the conventional view that
electoral competition, especially in circumstances of two-
partism, necessarily impels parties to adopt similar programmes and to exclude many relevant, but secondary, issues
from political debate. The Conservative and Labour parties'
post-war political consensus did not fall from the skies.
Rather, as Burnham usefully reminds us, 'it was fashioned
under specific historical circumstances by specific leaders . . .
and maintained so long, and only so long, as the contexts were
favourable'.[45] Indeed, the major parties' policy consensus on
race and other issues that cut across party lines was founded
on two specific, ephemeral assumptions: appealing to floating
voters yielded greater electoral returns than satisfying core
supporters;[46] and electoral parity between the major parties
would persist indefinitely. By the late 1970s, these assumptions were undermined by political developments. In particular, the haemorrhaging of both major parties' partisan and
electoral support, and the increasing inability of Labour to
secure a working parliamentary majority threw the parties
back on to core constituencies antagonistic to consensual
politics. [47] In the general movement toward adversarial politics,
inter-party conflict and competition on race were renewed.[48]

---

[44] Downs, op. cit., p. 68.

[45] Walter Dean Burnham, 'Great Britain: The Death of the Collectivist Consensus?', in Louis Maisel and Joseph Cooper (eds.), *Political Parties*, Beverly Hills,
CA, Sage, 1977, p. 268.

[46] Gamble, op. cit., p. 101.

[47] See, e.g., Dennis Kavanagh (ed.), *The Politics of the Labour Party*, London, Allen
and Unwin, 1982; and Stuart Hall and Martin Jacques (eds.), *The Politics of
Thatcherism*, London, Lawrence and Wishart, 1983.

[48] For a brief discussion of the breakdown of the politics of consensus in Britain
and elsewhere see Brent Steel and Taketsugu Tsurutani, 'From Consensus to
Dissensus: A Note on Postindustrial Political Parties', *Comparative Politics*, 18.2, Jan.
1986, 235–48.

PLAN OF THE BOOK

In accordance with this general analysis of post-war politics in Britain, the following chapters can be divided into three parts: the evolution and implementation of the racial consensus of the parties, 1958–75 (Chapters 2, 3, 4); the erosion of consensus, 1975–80 (Chapter 5); and the renewal of party competition on race, 1980–8 (Chapters 6, 7).

Chapter 2 traces the historical evolution of the racial consensus of the Conservative and Labour parties. To extricate race from politics the parties excluded race from inter-party debate and their electoral platforms, enacted anti-discrimination legislation in conjunction with increasingly restrictive immigration controls, and created and supported 'racial buffers' (quasi-governmental institutions designed to deflect race-related issues away from the parties and government).

Chapter 3 uses a survey of 40 Community Relations Councils (CRCs) to trace the historical relationship between these local bodies concerned with race and the major political parties. CRCs flourished in the 1960s as a consequence of the strategy of the parties to depoliticize race, and, hence, the character and orientation of these organizations primarily have been shaped by political forces. The work of CRCs was given explicit political direction at the national level by the buffer institutions which the parties had created; and, more directly, by local government. The success of the major parties in tying CRCs to government virtually ensured that these organizations would not challenge the parties' consensus on race.

Chapter 4 complements the discussion of CRCs with a profile of one racially troubled locality, the London borough of Ealing. A local case-study is useful because it is at the sub-national level where electoral and political pressures on the parties to address race-related problems would appear to be the most intense. Ealing is a particularly relevant case because neither the Conservative nor the Labour party is electorally dominant. The borough has had a history of racial conflict; and since non-whites make up more than a quarter of Ealing's total population, they are a highly visible group.

The political consequences of the neglect of race-related

issues by the parties are examined in Chapter 5. This chapter primarily focuses on two major protest movements, the National Front (NF) and the Anti-Nazi League (ANL), which emerged in the 1970s to challenge the parties' racial consensus. The popularity of groups as different as the NF and the ANL demonstrated voters' anxieties about race relations and immigration and dissatisfaction with the parties. Partly as a consequence of the activities and pressures of these groups, party competition on race was renewed.

The repoliticization of race is discussed in Chapter 6. Evidence from the author's questionnaire to MPs, interviews with party élites, and other sources indicate that the racial consensus has eroded on three fronts: race has re-emerged as an electoral issue; party-élite opinion on race-related questions has visibly diverged; and the race policies of the post-1979 Conservative Governments have been opposed by the Opposition. These developments contrast with the 1964–75 period when consensus on race-related public policy prevailed among Conservative and Labour party élites.

Chapter 7 analyses two consequences of renewed party competition on race: the achievement of non-white political voice within the Labour party and the political mobilization of Labour's ethnic-minority activists. This chapter specifically focuses on the current controversy over the proposal for the adoption of 'black sections'.

2
Political Consensus and the Depoliticization of Race

INTRODUCTION

The emergence of race as a political variable in Britain after 1958 raised serious difficulties for those agents principally responsible for formulating and articulating racial public policy: the major political parties. How the Conservative and Labour parties reacted to these difficulties, the motivations underlying their responses, and the political context in which these responses were formulated are the central concerns of this chapter.

The central argument presented here is that the sharp, intra-party divisions which the race issue engendered after 1958 and the persistence of strong illiberal public opinion on the subject motivated Conservative and Labour leaders to attempt to extricate race from British politics. They pursued this objective by denying that race was a salient political issue, by enacting cosmetic anti-discrimination legislation in conjunction with ever more restrictive immigration controls, and by creating and politically supporting racial buffers. Together, these distinct but interwoven strategies were implemented to cultivate what Conservative and Labour leaders sought most after 1964: an intra- and inter-party consensus on race-related issues. The essence of this consensus was that race would play no significant role in the parties' contest for office.

THE ORIGINS OF RACE AS A POLITICAL ISSUE

While pervading most public policy, the heart of the post-war consensus was the fundamental agreement between the major parties on the means and ends of managing the economy.[1] In a post-war Britain starved of cheap labour, the convergence of their economic strategy meant that both parties were not strongly opposed to the arrival of New Commonwealth workers to man Britain's underutilized factories.[2] Peach has demonstrated that West Indian migration ebbed and flowed in more or less automatic harmony with fluctuations in Britain's economy.[3] Other studies suggest that New Commonwealth migratory patterns were principally governed by the demand for unskilled labour in Britain rather than the 'push' of unstable economic conditions in the sending countries.[4] The migration of New Commonwealth workers was facilitated politically by the passage of the 1948 British Nationality Act which granted full British citizenship, including the right of unrestricted entry into Britain, to all Commonwealth citizens. Capitalizing on these opportunities, more than 200,000 Indian, Pakistani, and West Indian nationals entered Britain as migrant workers or permanent settlers between 1955 and 1960.

Not surprisingly, the influx of approximately a quarter of a million non-white immigrants over a relatively short period strained social services in local areas where immigrants settled. Particularly in inner-city districts, severe health, educational, and housing problems arose virtually overnight. As Foot explains:

The local councils had no estimate from the central government of the numbers coming to their area, no guidance from the Health or Education Ministries on the possibilities of different health and sanitation standards or on the difficulties of teaching children who could not speak English.[5]

[1] See A. M. Gamble and S. A. Walkland, *The British Party System and Economic Policy 1945–83*, Oxford, OUP, 1984, pp. 1–93.
[2] A. Sivanandan, 'Race, Class and the State: The Black Experience in Britain', London, Institute of Race Relations, 1976. The Labour party supported unrestricted immigration despite the initial reservations of many trade unions and rank and file trade unionists.
[3] G. C. K. Peach, *West Indian Migration to Britain*, London, OUP, 1968.
[4] See K. Jones and A. D. Smith, *The Economic Impact of Commonwealth Migration*, London, CUP, 1970.
[5] Paul Foot, *Immigration and Race in British Politics*, Harmondsworth, Penguin, 1965, p. 162.

Unlike the French post-war experience, immigration into Britain after 1951 was unplanned.[6] Receiving little financial assistance from central government, local authorities bore most of the economic costs of this migration.

Despite these difficulties, the major parties at the national level could avoid race-related issues because they were peripheral to the daily lives of most citizens. Between 1948 and 1961 racial problems were 'raised only sporadically in the House of Commons and never by the Government or Opposition front benches'.[7] The essence of this pre-political condition, as Katznelson has described it, was the benign neglect of race-related difficulties by the parties. 'That there were any problems of discrimination, prejudice, integration, and social deficiences, was implicitly denied'.[8] For most of this period the parties assumed that problems arising from non-white immigration would be resolved by existing welfare bodies or by voluntary immigrant advisory agencies then emerging locally.[9] Complacent in this view, neither party explicitly addressed race-related issues nor exploited the subject for political advantage.

This pre-political state of affairs was eventually disturbed by the violent racial clashes which occurred in Nottingham and Notting Hill in the summer of 1958. As a consequence of these separate incidents, race was propelled—if only temporarily—to the forefront of national public attention. The disturbances fundamentally altered the politics of race in two respects: they provided political ammunition for the handful of Conservative MPs then clamouring for immigration controls [10] and they rudely introduced thousands of previously indifferent citizens to the problems associated with New Commonwealth immigration. Although race-related issues were not prominent in the 1959 general election, the disturbances highlighted the government's lack of explicit policy on immigration. Moreover, public anxiety over non-white immigration in the affected constituencies helped to elect a

[6] See Gary P. Freeman, *Immigrant Labor and Racial Conflict in Industrial Societies*, Princeton, NJ, Princeton Univ. Press, 1979.

[7] Ira Katznelson, *Black Men, White Cities*, London, OUP, 1973, p. 126.

[8] Ibid., p. 127.

[9] See Ch. 3 for further discussion of this point.

[10] For a brief account of the activities of this group see Foot, op. cit., pp. 124–36.

number of illiberal Conservative parliamentary candidates, thereby strengthening that party's anti-immigrant lobby.

Anti-immigrant sentiment at this time was especially prevalent among Conservative activists. The near-hysteria of the local constituencies over the number of non-whites entering the country was evident, for example, in the 39 anti-immigration resolutions forwarded to the 1961 Annual Conservative Party Conference. The following resolutions reflect activist opinion at the Conservative grass roots:

That this Conference, having regard to the effects of uncontrolled immigration on some parts of the country and to the growing weight of public opinion that there should be some measure of control, urges the government to take such steps at the earliest possible time as it considers appropriate, both to reduce the extent of immigration and to secure a wider dispersal of immigrants.

This Conference urges the government to reconsider the immigration laws as they now stand, and institute controls whereby all immigrants, prior to being permitted entry, satisfy the authorities that they have reasonable means of support and prospects of work; and also urges that medical examination be compulsory for all, in order to safeguard the health of this country.[11]

The involvement of local Conservative activists with extra-parliamentary, anti-immigrant organizations, such as the Birmingham Immigration Control Association, further impressed the Macmillan government with the intensity of grass-roots anti-immigrant sentiment.[12] Responding to this, as well as to pressures from vocal, anti-immigrant MPs, the Conservative government in 1961 moved to restrict New Commonwealth immigration.[13]

The reluctant decision of the government partially to close the door on Commonwealth immigration was not endorsed, however, by most of the Conservative party. Conservatives clustered around three distinct poles of opinion on race. The first group, which Foot has labelled Tory Radicals, defended an open Commonwealth immigration policy on economic grounds. From their perspective, non-white immigrants made an important contribution to Britain's manufacturing and

---

[11] *Conservative Party Conference Agenda 1961*, London, Conservative party, pp. 10–11.
[12] Foot, op. cit., pp. 195–200.
[13] Katznelson, op. cit., p. 134.

service industries which, if terminated, might precipitate labour shortages and jeopardize economic growth. Since New Commonwealth workers were vital to Britain's economy, less effort should be expended on restricting their numbers than on integrating those already resident. Advocates of government assisted integration measures, including anti-discrimination legislation, were especially prevalent in Parliament where they were an influential pressure group.[14]

A second faction aimed to preserve some semblance of Britain's former Empire. Internationally orientated, this group included Conservative politicians who had lived in Britain's former colonies and whose attachment to the Commonwealth ideal impelled many to 'speak up for the people they have governed'.[15] According to Foot, an informal alliance between this group and the Tory Radicals blocked parliamentary initiatives to restrict immigration in the late 1950s.[16] Once the 1962 Commonwealth Immigrants Act was passed, however, many in this faction accepted the entry restrictions and focused on integration measures aimed at ensuring racial harmony.

The third Conservative faction on race—what Gamble has called the new Right—opposed non-white immigration virtually from its inception.[17] Articulating the views of the Tory professional middle class, this group was poorly represented in Parliament and, until the early 1960s, not very influential. The political base of the new Right was located in the constituencies; through its efforts the numerous anti-immigration resolutions were forwarded to the 1961 and 1965 Conservative Party Conferences. The political influence of this faction was enhanced over time by two events: the 1958 street disturbances; and the Smethwick fiasco at the general election of 1964, which will be discussed below. Foot, for one, argues that political lobbying by this faction was instrumental in bringing about the 1962 Commonwealth Immigrants Act.[18]

Public opinion indisputably was sympathetic to the views of

[14] Foot, op. cit., p. 154.
[15] Ibid., p. 155.
[16] Ibid., pp. 129-38.
[17] Andrew Gamble, *The Conservative Nation*, London, Routledge, 1974.
[18] Foot, op. cit., pp. 153-8.

the control lobby over those of the Radicals and Common-wealth Idealists. By 1961 the public favoured immigration restrictions by a margin of more than six to one (see Table 2.1). Moreover, despite the limited exposure of most Britons to race-related difficulties, public opinion toward already settled non-whites was illiberal too.[19] Of particular political

TABLE 2.1. *Public opinion on New Commonwealth immigration, 1961–1966 (% of respondents)*

(1) 1961: *Do you approve or disapprove of the measures the government intends to take in controlling immigration from Commonwealth countries?*

(*a*)	Approve	76
(*b*)	Disapprove	12
(*c*)	Don't know	12

(2) 1961: *Do you think that coloured people from the Commonwealth should have the right of completely free entry into Britain, should there be restrictions on entry, or should they be kept out completely?*

(*a*)	Free entry	21
(*b*)	Restriction	67
(*c*)	Kept out completely	6
(*d*)	Don't know	6

(3) *Do you think that too many immigrants have been let into the country or not?*

		1963	1964	1966
(*a*)	Too many	84	81	81
(*b*)	Not too many	12	13	14
(*c*)	Don't know	4	6	5

Sources: David Butler and Donald Stokes, *Political Change in Britain*, 2nd edn., New York, St. Martin's, 1974, Table 14.7; *The Gallup International Public Opinion Polls, Great Britain, 1937–75*, New York, Random House, 1976.

[19] See Catherine Jones, *Immigration and Social Policy in Britain*, London, Tavistock, 1977, pp. 133–54.

significance were the results of a 1960 survey of 604 manual workers and their dependants which revealed that public opposition to non-white immigration cross-cut partisan boundaries.[20]

Given the breadth of public opposition to non-white immigration and its own internal divisions on the subject, the Macmillan government proposed the 1962 Immigrants Act to effect a compromise between the restrictionist lobby and the defenders of the Commonwealth. It did so by looking two ways at once on immigration. On the one hand the Act severely curtailed primary immigration by instituting a labour-voucher system. This provision sharply reduced the number of workers entering Britain from 50,000 plus during the Act's first six months of implementation in 1962 to approximately 13,000 for the whole of 1965 (see Table 2.2). However, to placate the defenders of the Commonwealth, the Act allowed the entry of the dependants of workers, hence unintentionally precipitating 'a movement of workers, many of whom intended to stay temporarily, into a permanent immigration of families'.[21] Indeed, while 57,710 labourers entered Britain between 1963 and 1965, almost twice as many dependants were admitted for settlement during this period,

TABLE 2.2. *Commonwealth immigration into Britain, 1962–1965*

Year	Holders of Labour Ministry Vouchers	Dependants
July–Dec. 1962	51,121	8,832
1963	30,125	26,234
1964	14,705	37,460
1965	12,880	41,214

Source: David Butler and Anne Sloman, *British Political Facts 1900–79*, London, Macmillan, 1980, p. 300.

[20] R. T. McKenzie and A. Silver, *Angels in Marble*, London, Heinemann, 1968, p. 152.
[21] Steven Castles and Godula Kosack, *Immigrant Workers and Class Structure in Western Europe*, London, OUP, 1973, p. 31.

thereby increasing aggregate New Commonwealth immigration by 73 per cent over the period of no restrictions.[22] Contrary to the intentions of the control lobby, rumours of possible future entry barriers, and their widespread circulation in the New Commonwealth, precipitated more immigration into Britain between 1960 and 1962 than in all previous years combined. In addition to increasing overall immigration, moreover, the debate over restrictions heightened public awareness of the race issue, thereby compounding the Conservative party's difficulties in resolving its internal divisions quietly.

LABOUR'S RESPONSE: PARTISAN CONFLICT AND INTERNAL DIVISIONS

The problems of the Conservative leadership were further exacerbated by the Labour party's unexpected and virulent opposition to entry barriers. The resistance of Labour in Parliament to the 1961 Immigration Bill effectively concluded the pre-political period by ushering in a period of partisan conflict over race. In a forceful speech, the Labour leader Hugh Gaitskell described the Act during its second reading as a 'miserable, shameful, shabby bill' which demonstrated the Conservative government's lack of confidence in Britain's ability to 'absorb or integrate with our community more than 1 per cent of the population'.[23] In challenging the claim of the government that restrictions would significantly improve British race relations, Gaitskell asked rhetorically:

Do the government deal with [the problem] by seeking to combat social evils, by building more houses and enforcing laws against overcrowding, by using every educational means at their disposal to create tolerance and mutual understanding, and by emphasizing . . . the value of the immigrants and setting their face firmly against all forms of racial intolerance and discrimination?[24]

---

[22] See David Butler and Ann Sloman, *British Political Facts 1900–79*, London, Macmillan, 1980, pp. 298–300.
[23] As quoted in, Katznelson, op. cit., p. 136.
[24] As quoted in Freeman, op. cit., pp. 51–2.

So forcefully did Labour present its case against controls that, according to Studlar, its 'opposition to the 1961 Immigration Bill can be considered the major factor in lowering the percentage of people supporting the bill from 76 per cent in early November that year to 62 per cent in December'.[25] Even the Conservative Home Secretary R. A. Butler acknowledged that Gaitskell's speech had placed the Conservative front bench on the political defensive.[26]

Why did Labour oppose the introduction of controls so strongly? Why did Labour's parliamentary leaders adopt what they undoubtedly knew was an unpopular position among its white working-class supporters? The actions of the Labour party can be best understood in the context of its internal divisions on race. Like its political opposition, Labour split into three factions, with two opposed to immigration restrictions.

The first group of Labour Radicals, of which Gaitskell was the leading spokesman, was virtually indistinguishable from its Conservative counterpart. This faction too appreciated the economic return of non-white immigration and it strongly opposed measures which could precipitate adverse economic consequences. A second faction, the traditional Left, held many of the same views as the Conservative Idealists. The Left valued the preservation of the Commonwealth even at the expense of domestic social unrest. Among all groups the Left alone had been advocating anti-discrimination legislation since the 1950s. Along with the Radicals the Left supported Gaitskell's opposition to the 1961 Commonwealth Immigrants Bill.

Labour's conservative Right was opposed to both these groups. A minority voice before 1963, the Right opposed non-white immigration principally on racial grounds.[27] For the Right, racial prejudice often combined with electoral considerations in what can best be described as a 'little England' perspective on immigration. Central to that outlook was the belief that, irrespective of the economic benefits to be derived

[25] Donley T. Studlar, 'British Public Opinion, Colour Issues and Enoch Powell: A Longitudinal Analysis', *British Journal of Political Science*, 4.3, July 1974, 371–81.

[26] Katznelson, op. cit., pp. 136–8.

[27] Foot, op. cit., p. 190.

from continued New Commonwealth immigration, non-
whites could not be easily absorbed into English society.
Although the Right enjoyed considerable support among
Labour voters, especially in local areas directly affected by
immigration, its views were not endorsed by most Labour
activists. In contrast to the Conservative party, anti-
immigration pressure from Labour's constituency branches,
at least up to 1964, was not strong.[28]

Without such grass-roots pressure Labour's national
leaders were relatively free to oppose immigration restrictions.
Unfettered immigration was, on the whole, popular within the
parliamentary party and consistent with the socialist principles over which Labour had fought so bitterly in the autumn
of 1961.[29] Moreover, despite the anxieties of the party's right
wing, race had not emerged as a national, electoral issue
before 1961 and there was little reason to believe it would do
so in the future. In short, Labour appeared to have little to
lose politically, and perhaps something to gain, by opposing
restrictions on moral grounds. At least one observer has
suggested the leadership used the emotional debate over
immigration to rally its badly demoralized supporters, then
reeling from Labour's third consecutive general-election
defeat.[30]

Whatever their initial motives, the leaders of the party did
not sustain their opposition to immigration controls for very
long. Once the 1962 Commonwealth Immigrants Act was
enacted, Labour's objections to entry restrictions were notice-
ably less vocal, with even Gaitskell apparently resigned to the
implementation of controls. The diminished enthusiasm of the
Labour leadership for free entry undoubtedly was linked to
the continued unpopularity of non-white immigration among
the public, and specifically within the white working class.
Despite Labour's efforts in 1961, public opinion remained
overwhelmingly in favour of restrictions and illiberal toward

[28] The constituencies were to the left of the parliamentary party on immigration.
See *Report of the Annual Conference 1965*, London, Labour party, pp. 212–20 for the
furore created by the publication of the White Paper, *Immigration from the
Commonwealth*.

[29] These battles revolved around clause IV of the Labour party constitution which
commits the party to the objective of bringing about socialism.

[30] Katznelson, op. cit., pp. 135–8.

already settled ethnic minorities.[31] Moreover, some observers claim that other political issues soon diverted Labour's attention. By 1963, it has been argued, the party was too busy preparing for an impending general election to be concerned with what many activists believed was the electorally marginal race issue.[32]

While perhaps accounting for Labour's lack of interest in the immigration question, the above argument does not explain the subsequent adoption of a restrictionist posture by the party in 1964. Labour's sudden turn-about was evident in the party's 1964 election manifesto which bluntly argued that the 'number of immigrants entering the United Kingdom must be limited'.[33] In promising that a Labour government would 'retain immigration control' until a 'satisfactory agreement covering . . . [immigration] could be negotiated with the Commonwealth',[34] the party effectively endorsed the entry restrictions it had opposed less than three years earlier. Although its policy reversal was tempered by manifesto commitments to legislate against racial discrimination and to aid 'local authorities in areas where immigrants have settled',[35] there is little doubt about Labour's principal focus. The inclusion of the above pledge under the heading 'Commonwealth Immigration' reflected Labour's association of domestic race-related problems with the number of non-whites entering Britain. As we have seen above, the Conservative party initially had suggested this link in 1961.

Why did the Labour party suddenly reverse itself on immigration? Apart from the obvious influence of illiberal public opinion, Katznelson and others point to the significance of Gaitskell's unexpected death in January 1963.[36] Gaitskell had been Labour's principal advocate of unfettered immigration. With his death, Deakin argues, the 'main driving force of the Labour opposition to immigration controls

[31] See Studlar, op. cit., on this point.
[32] See Nicholas Deakin, 'The Politics of the Commonwealth Immigrants Bill', *Political Quarterly*, 39.1, Jan.–Mar. 1968, 25–45.
[33] F. W. S. Craig (ed.), *British General Election Manifestos 1900–74*, London, Macmillan, 1975, p. 268.
[34] Ibid.
[35] Ibid.
[36] Katznelson, op. cit,. p 144.

disappeared', creating the opportunity for a shift in policy under the new leadership of Harold Wilson. [37] Given the persistence of illiberal sentiment within the electorate and the anticipation of a general election by 1964, Deakin believes that Labour compromised its former progressive posture to avoid alienating white voters.[38] Thus Labour's racial policy largely converged with that of its political opposition.[39]

Since little had changed on the immigration front since 1961, apart from Gaitskell's death, clearly something had influenced Labour to support restrictions. But was the party's change of immigration policy motivated simply by short-term electoral considerations? Had the balance of political influence within the Labour party remained unchanged until 1964, especially on race, this may have been the entire story. However, Labour's internal political alignments were not static. Earlier Labour had divided on race along three axes of opinion with the Radicals and the Left prevailing in favour of unfettered immigration, but between 1962 and 1964 a fourth faction emerged representing the pragmatic centre. Led by MPs Richard Crossman, Roy Hattersley, Frank Soskice, and the Labour leader Harold Wilson, the Centrists viewed race as a politically volatile issue which Labour should avoid. In harmony with the Conservative Right, this faction supported entry restrictions to allay the xenophobia of the electorate. Unlike the Right, however, the Centrists were not racially prejudiced nor convinced that the race issue could be resolved easily. Rather, race was a political joker that not only could impede Labour from immediately gaining power but, also, and perhaps more importantly, deflect the party from its post–1951 adherence to centrist, non-ideological politics. As the Housing Minister Richard Crossman implicitly revealed in his diary comments of August 1965, such a

[37] Deakin, op. cit., p. 42.

[38] A straw poll conducted by the shadow cabinet in the summer of 1963 found most MPs in favour of breaking away from the Gaitskell position. According to Howard, the poll results 'confirmed the worst foreboding in the shadow cabinet that opinion on the issue had shifted alarmingly' since 1961. Anthony Howard, 'The Skin Game', *New Statesman*, 33, 22 Nov. 1963.

[39] A compromise statement written by Wilson accepting the case for controls in the autumn of 1963 was adopted by the PLP by 85 votes to 5, indicating the parliamentary party's retreat from 1961. Katznelson, op. cit., p. 145.

scenario was precisely what the Centrists sought to avoid:

This afternoon we had the Statement on immigration and the publication of the White Paper. This has been one of the most difficult and unpleasant jobs the Government has had to do. We have become illiberal and lowered the quotas at a time when we have an acute shortage of labour. ... I can't overestimate the shock to the Party. This will confirm the feeling that ours is not a socialist Government, that it is surrendering to pressure, that it is not in control of its own destiny. ... When you add immigration to Vietnam you realize why the rank and file feel that we have abandoned our pledges and are retreating from socialism. The White Paper will probably have a deeper undermining effect on the moral strength of Harold Wilson's leadership than any other thing that we have done.[40]

Crossman well understood that Labour's new policy on race was part of a larger centrist strategy, a strategy which was abhorrent to the party's Left but fundamental to the Centrists' ambitions for national office. The deepest political conviction of this faction was that Labour could only become the majority party in Britain by capturing the so-called political middle ground.[41]

Pursuit of the political middle ground motivated the Centrists, and particularly Wilson, to avoid all policy commitments which might unnecessarily polarize public opinion along partisan lines. Such a course was part of Labour's strategy to 'project a more contemporary, classless image than in the past', as 'the party sought to be regarded as efficient, energetic and up-to-date—concerned with "the problems of the 60s" and "the new Britain" '.[42] With respect to race this meant adopting the stance of its political opposition on the issue. As Crossman put it: 'We felt we had to out-trump the Tories by doing what they would have done and so transforming their policy into a bipartisan policy.'[43] The decision to reverse the party's 1961 posture was not widely

[40] Richard Crossman, *The Diaries of a Cabinet Minister Volume I 1964–66*, New York, Holt, Rinehart and Winston, 1975, p. 299.

[41] See Ralph Miliband, *Parliamentary Socialism*, London, Merlin Press, 1979, pp. 350–77.

[42] David Butler and Anthony King, *The British General Election of 1964*, New York, St. Martin's, 1965.

[43] Crossman, op. cit., p. 299.

debated, as Labour's National Executive Committee decided only at the last moment to include a promise to retain immigration control in the party's 1964 general-election manifesto.[44] Such indecisiveness reflected the ambivalence of the new leadership on race. Although it intended to repudiate the former posture of the party on immigration, it did not wish to publicize its decision. Thus, Labour's about-face on immigration should be viewed less as a well-considered policy reversal than an attempt by the Wilson leadership to defuse a potentially divisive issue. By aligning itself with its political opposition Wilson hoped to avoid assuming a posture on immigration that would require a public defence.

SMETHWICK AND THE EXACERBATION OF POLITICAL TENSIONS

Despite the efforts of the Centrists, however, race did emerge as a political issue during the 1964 general-election campaign as a result of the traumatic events which occurred in the industrial Midlands borough of Smethwick. In the local campaign Labour's shadow foreign secretary Patrick Gordon Walker MP lost his seat to Peter Griffiths, a Conservative maverick who explicitly courted anti-immigrant votes by raising the spectre of 'voters in their turbans and saris' deciding the future of Smethwick.[45] Griffiths gained a political advantage by highlighting Gordon Walker's outspoken opposition to the 1962 Immigrants Act and his apparent indifference to the impact of immigration on Smethwick's local economy.[46] The Smethwick outcome substantially raised the visibility of the race issue nationally because of the ferocity of the contest and Griffiths' victory over one of Labour's prominent leaders in the face of a national pro-Labour swing. The subsequent defeat of Gordon Walker at the Leyton by-election in January 1965 only further politicized the issue.

The extent to which the electoral outcome at Smethwick altered the major parties', and especially Labour's, perception

---

[44] Butler and King, op. cit.
[45] Foot, op. cit., p. 46.
[46] Ibid., pp. 63–79.

of the race issue cannot be overstated. In a statement of unusual acerbity and in breach of parliamentary protocol, the newly elected Labour Prime Minister Harold Wilson attacked Griffiths in the opening address of the Queen's speech:

Is the Leader of the Opposition proud of his hon. friend the Member for Smethwick? Does he now intend to take him to his bosom? Will the Conservative whip be extended to him, because if he does accept him as a colleague he will make this clear: he will betray the principles which not only his party but also his nation have hitherto had the right to proclaim.[47]

Venting anger at Griffiths for manipulating the race issue for political advantage, Wilson described the freshman Member as a 'parliamentary leper' who would be returned to 'oblivion' at the next general election.[48] The unprecedented tone of Wilson's remarks coupled with the ambivalence of the Tory front bench toward Griffiths indicate the turmoil which the Smethwick campaign had visited on both major parties.[49] Whatever posture the parties adopted on Griffiths' campaign, the race issue would only be further propelled into the political limelight. Although this end was consistent with the objectives of Labour in 1961, three years later it was something both the Conservative and Labour leaderships preferred to avoid. In the words of Richard Crossman, race had become by 1964 the 'hottest potato in politics'.[50]

Smethwick and the demise of the pre-political state of affairs on race presented the major parties with a thorny dilemma. For the Conservatives, the dilemma was how to reconcile its internal divisions on race while simultaneously presenting a united front to a predominantly illiberal electorate. As we have seen above, the failure of the 1962 Immigrants Act to resolve this dilemma—indeed its role in exacerbating it—left the Conservative party more divided than it was before the passage of the Act. The thirty-one resolutions advocating further restrictions at the 1965 Conservative Party Conference in conjunction with the

---

[47] Ibid., pp. 65–6.
[48] Ibid., p. 66.
[49] Many Conservative MPs were shocked by Wilson's attack on Griffiths and the leader of the Opposition refused to comment on Griffiths' campaign.
[50] Crossman, op. cit., p. 149.

parliamentary success in the same year of a Tory private member's bill calling for 'precise limits' on immigration highlighted the inadequacy of the leadership's 1962 efforts.[51] Three years after the implementation of entry controls, the party was still beset by many of the same pressures which motivated the Macmillan government to opt for restrictions. The Labour party was hardly more united. According to Freeman:

> The dilemma confronted in Transport House by the leaders of the Labour party was more complicated if less serious. They faced a rebellion by the working class if they persisted in a strongly pro-immigrant policy and a defection by the socialist-intellectual Left if they opted for controls. For them . . . the less said about the subject, the less intense public opinion, the better.[52]

The Labour party's dilemma was exacerbated by its assumption of power in 1964, when the Wilson government was confronted with the unattractive alternatives of either further tightening controls or being perceived by a substantial percentage of the electorate to be acting irresponsibly. As Richard Crossman summarized this problem:

> Ever since the Smethwick election it has been quite clear that immigration can be the greatest potential vote-loser for the Labour party if we are seen to be permitting a flood of immigrants to come in and blight the central areas in all our cities.[53]

Smethwick also highlighted the potential peril of not addressing oneself to the race issue to the satisfaction of the electorate. Labour's promise in the manifesto to retain immigration restrictions had apparently had little effect in Smethwick or in the country as a whole because of the reluctance of the party to raise the issue during the election campaign.[54]

FORGING A BIPARTISAN CONSENSUS

The response of the parties to the politicization of race at Smethwick was to extricate the subject from the political

---

[51] Katznelson, op. cit., pp. 147–8.　　　　[52] Freeman, op. cit., p. 112.
[53] Crossman, op. cit., pp. 149–50.
[54] Foot implies that Gordon Walker too was in favour of restrictions by 1964, but was reluctant to say so in public during the general election, op. cit., pp. 159–62.

arena.[55] Between 1964 and 1975 the Conservative and Labour leaders followed an informal rule of avoiding race-related subjects. While this agreement endured, the party in government—whether Conservative or Labour—could expect the Opposition to co-operate in this area to an extent rarely enjoyed on other issues. For over a decade, British race policy was truly bipartisan.

Like most policy consensus the understanding of the Conservative and Labour parties on race evolved incrementally. Its essential outlines were initially set forth in the Labour government's 1965 White Paper on immigration which sought to control the entry of immigrants and create 'positive measures designed to secure for immigrants and their children their rightful place' in British society.[56] To secure the first objective the White Paper proposed to reduce the issue of work-vouchers to Commonwealth citizens from 20,000 to 8,500 annually, and to accept only those immigrants with demonstrable skills or professional qualifications. To realize the second objective the White Paper established a National Committee for Commonwealth Immigrants (NCCI) 'to co-ordinate on a national basis efforts directed towards the integration of Commonwealth immigrants into the community'.[57] The latter aim was in theory facilitated by the Labour government's introduction of the 1965 Race Relations Act, which 'prohibited "incitement of racial hatred", called for the use of conciliation measures to deal with offenses, and set up a Race Relations Board to administer the law'.[58] Passage of the Act ostensibly fulfilled Labour's 1964 manifesto commitment to legislate against racial discrimination.

The co-operation of the Conservative party in parliamentary committee in drafting the Act and its acceptance of the general outlines of Labour's White Paper visibly reflected the new bipartisanship on race. The Conservative leader Douglas-Home personally characterized Labour's initiatives

---

[55] At one stage during the 1970 general election, Richard Crossman revealed that the Conservative and Labour parties had a tacit understanding not to exploit the race issue for electoral advantage. See Nicholas Deakin and Jenny Bourne, 'Powell, the Minorities and the 1970 Election', *Political Quarterly*, 41.4, Oct.–Dec. 1970, 399–415.

[56] As cited in, Katznelson, op. cit, p. 142.

[57] Ibid.

[58] Freeman, op. cit., p. 54.

on race relations as 'sensible and very fair'.[59] Norman St
John-Stevas, the Conservative Radical, cited the 'broad area
of agreement on this [immigration] question. . . . We are all
agreed on the need for control.'[60] Katznelson argues that in its
final, diluted version, the Race Relations Act was acceptable
to a vast majority of MPs.[61] The essence of this consensus,
however, was perhaps best summarized by the Labour
Centrist Roy Hattersley who declared in a 1965 parliamentary
address:

We are all in favour of some sort of limitation. We all wholeheartedly oppose any sort of discrimination. We all wholeheartedly
agree that there should be assimilation or adjustment, whichever
word one prefers to use. Those three points of view characterise the
view and principles of both major parties.[62]

Although Hattersley undoubtedly exaggerated the point,
there is little doubt that by December 1965 considerable inter-
party agreement existed in this policy area. This consensus
could be summed up in a concise phrase: keep race out of
party politics.

THE DEPOLITICIZATION OF RACE

(i) Conspiracies of silence

The least effective and simplest strategy the major parties
pursued to depoliticize race-related issues was to deny that
they were politically relevant. As several commentators have
noted, the silence of the parties on race was most conspicuous
during election campaigns.[63] During the 1964 general
election, for instance, only 8 Conservative, 14 Labour, and 3
Liberal parliamentary candidates mentioned immigration or
race relations in their campaign addresses despite, as we saw
in Chapter 1, the salience of these issues within the electorate.

---

[59] As cited in, Katznelson, op. cit., p. 149.
[60] Ibid., p. 141.
[61] Ibid., p. 149.
[62] Ibid., p. 141.
[63] See Donley T. Studlar, 'The Impact of the Colored Immigration Issue on
British Electoral Politics', Ph.D. dissertation, Indiana University, 1975.

This trend continued: immigration was cited in the election addresses of only 6 per cent of all parliamentary candidates in 1966 and 14 per cent in 1970 (see Table 2.3). Labour candidates were especially reluctant to address themselves to the immigration issue: between 1966 and October 1974 no more than 2 per cent mentioned the subject in their campaign statements, with no candidates discussing it in 1966 and 1970. Although the national manifestos of the parties cited this area more frequently, such discussions were often purposely vague.[64] Neither party made prior mention, for the most part, of the Race Relations and Immigration Acts which each would subsequently introduce in office. As we shall see below, even the passage of these bills through Parliament usually generated little partisan debate.

An exception to this conspiracy of silence was, of course, Enoch Powell's campaign from 1968 to 1974 against non-white immigration, a campaign which consisted of a series of inflammatory speeches, in which Powell attacked the leaders

TABLE 2.3. *Parliamentary candidates mentioning immigration in their general-election addresses, 1964–1974* (%)

Year	Conservative	Labour	Liberal
1964	8	14	3
1966	11	0	0
1970	26	0	n/a
1974 (Feb.)	6	1	1
1974 (Oct.)	10	2	2

Sources: David Butler and Anthony King, *The British General Election of 1964*, New York, St. Martin's, 1965; David Butler and Anthony King, *The British General Election of 1966*, New York, St. Martin's 1966; David Butler and Michael Pinto-Duschinsky, *The British General Election of 1970*, New York, St. Martin's, 1971; David Butler and Dennis Kavanagh, *The British General Election of February 1974*, London, Macmillan, 1974; David Butler and Dennis Kavanagh, *The British General Election of October 1974*, London, Macmillan, 1975.

[64] Labour's discussion of this area in the 1966 election manifesto is especially illustrative. See Craig, op. cit., p. 308.

of both major parties for ignoring the concerns of white Britons. In April 1968 Powell declared:

Those whom the gods wish to destroy, they first make mad. We must be mad, literally mad, as a nation to be permitting the annual inflow of some 50,000 dependants who are for the most part the material of the future growth of the immigrant-descended population. It is like watching a nation busily engaged in heaping up its own funeral pyre. . . . As I look ahead, I am filled with foreboding. Like the Roman, I seem to see 'the River Tiber foaming with much blood.'[65]

Powell's inflammatory anti-immigrant rhetoric, although an exception to the rule of silence, did not undermine the adherence of the Conservative party to this strategy. For Powell's remarks, while reflecting the sentiments of several senior colleagues, were not endorsed by the shadow cabinet.[66] Moreover, by removing Powell from the shadow cabinet in 1968, ostensibly for his intemperate remarks, Conservative leader Edward Heath effectively disassociated the Conservative leadership from Powell's views. But Powell's popularity within the electorate can be attributed to his dissention from official Conservative policy.[67]

It was not Powell's opinions which lost him favour with Heath and other Conservative leaders but the fact that he had expressed them publicly. In a statement which followed his announcement that Powell had been dropped from the shadow cabinet, Heath made it clear that he did not disagree with the substance of Powell's speech of April 1968: 'I have repeatedly emphasized that the policy of the Conservative party is that immigration must be more stringently limited and that immigrants wishing to return to their own countries should be helped financially to do so.'[68] What Heath apparently had objected to was the fact that Powell had violated the rule of silence. Heath's strategy on the subject was to promote quietly the need for further immigration

---

[65] As quoted in, David Butler and Michael Pinto-Duschinsky, *The British General Election of 1970*, New York, St. Martin's, 1971, pp. 76–7.

[66] Powell was inclined to speak out on a number of issues outside his responsibility. See Douglas E. Schoen, *Enoch Powell and the Powellites*, New York, St. Martin's, 1977, pp. 16–18.

[67] Ibid., pp. 160–97.

[68] As cited in, Katznelson, op. cit., p. 181.

restrictions without addressing the consequences of such restrictions for previously settled ethnic-minority families. Inflammatory talk of repatriating immigrants could possibly harm the electoral chances of the Conservative party by rekindling its internal divisions on race; hence, Powell's removal by Heath from the shadow cabinet.

The reluctance of Labour to challenge Powell's views, as it undoubtedly would have done under Gaitskell's leadership only a few years before, highlights the difficulties Powell created for *both* major parties.[69] As problematic as it was for Labour between elections, public discussion of the race issue was especially threatening to the party during electoral campaigns, as Richard Crossman implicitly reveals in his diary observations following Labour's 1966 election victory:

We had had the courage to publish the Immigration White Paper in 1965, which was bitterly attacked by every level. But it had worked—it had taken the poison out of politics so that in the 1966 election immigration was no longer a political issue.[70]

With specific reference to Powell, Butler and Pinto-Duschinsky argue:

Both sides were anxious about Mr. Powell. The Labour party feared with good reason that he excited some sympathy among their normal supporters, especially in the Midlands. The Conservatives knew that the Powell issue could divide their party down the middle; in both personal and ideological terms, most of the leadership was implacably opposed to him, but among the rank and file there were all too many who would say that Mr. Powell was their favourite Conservative.[71]

Conservative and Labour leaders primarily responded to Powellism by denying its relevance, a strategy which, as we will see in Chapter 5, had several adverse effects. In so doing, they lent legitimacy to Powell's assertion that he spoke for the British people on immigration.

---

[69] Apart from Tony Benn's personal attack on Powell during the 1970 election campaign, Labour did not make an issue of Powell's speeches and popularity.

[70] Richard Crossman, *The Diaries of a Cabinet Minister Volume II 1966–68*, New York, Holt, Rinehart, and Winston, 1976, p. 689.

[71] Butler and Pinto-Duschinsky, op. cit., p. 160.

(ii) Sending the electorate contradictory signals

The second strategy the parties pursued to depoliticize race was to enact cosmetic anti-discrimination legislation in conjunction with the implementation of further immigration controls. For every piece of restrictive immigration legislation adopted between 1965 and 1976, an accompanying race relations act either preceded or shortly followed its passage (see Table 2.4). Labour was especially adept at this game of political football; in 1965 and again in 1968 a Labour government successfully introduced both restrictive legislation and an anti-discrimination statute. The greater incongruity of Labour's race policy can probably be attributed to two factors: the party's longer tenure in office between 1965 and 1976; and more importantly, its stronger ideological commitment to combat racial discrimination through legislation. Although the 1965, 1968, and 1976 Race Relations Acts had considerable bipartisan support, each was vigorously contested by the Conservative new Right. To placate this wing of the party while not obstructing the legislative process, the Conservative front bench abstained during the third parliamentary readings of the 1968 and 1976 Acts.

By this strategy, the leaders of the major parties inextricably

TABLE 2.4. *Immigration and race-relations record of both major parties,*
1962–1976

Labour (in power)	Conservatives (in power)
Immigration White Paper 1965*	Commonwealth Immigrants Act 1962
Race Relations Act 1965	
Commonwealth Immigrants Act 1968	Immigration Act 1971
	Ugandan Asian Act 1972†
Race Relations Act 1968	
Race Relations Act 1976	

* Proposed both immigration controls and integrative measures.
† Allowed the entry of British passport holding Asians who had been expelled from Uganda by Idi Amin.

linked the subjects of race relations and non-white immigration. The major parties have long contended that restricting non-white immigration will free public authorities to cope with problems created by and affecting previously settled immigrants. Conservative policy-makers have often drawn this conclusion:

Good race relations are of immense importance. We are determined that all citizens shall continue to be treated as equal before the law, and without discrimination. . . . [Yet] local authority services are under great strain in many of the towns and cities where large numbers of immigrants have settled. . . . We will establish a single new system of control over all immigration from overseas. . . .

We will give assistance to Commonwealth immigrants who wish to return to their countries of origin, but we will not tolerate any attempt to harass or compel them to go against their will.[72]

The promotion of apparently contradictory legislation is only comprehensible when one considers that most race bills crystallized as a reaction to specific incidents of social unrest and/or the intensification of internal party divisions over race.[73] The genesis of the 1965 Race Relations Act for example can be traced to the fear of the parties that the 'Smethwick phenomenon' could become universal.[74] Other legislation too had its origins in the hasty reaction of the parties to immediate political pressures. Boston, for example, describes the 1968 Immigrants Act as a 'panic measure' intended to allay irrational fears of displaced Kenyan Asians flooding into Britain.[75] Rose argues generally that 'legislation on race relations in Britain has been characterized by a series of *ad hoc* and hasty government responses to specific and immediate controversies . . . the process . . . is far more complex and messy than that which is usually presented as characteristic of policy-making in modern British government'.[76]

[72] As cited in Studlar, 1975, p. 128.
[73] On this point see Keith Hindell, 'The Genesis of the Race Relations Bill', *Political Quarterly*, 36.4, Oct.–Dec. 1965, 390–405.
[74] Ibid., pp. 188–98.
[75] Richard Boston, 'How the Immigrants Act Was Passed', *New Society*, 11 Mar. 1968, 287.
[76] As cited in Hannan Rose, 'The Immigration Act 1971: A Case Study in the Work of Parliament', *Parliamentary Affairs*, 26.1, Winter 1972–3, 70–1.

Indeed, not only were the legislative initiatives of the parties on race up to 1976 *ad hoc*, but they were often secretive and inadequately debated. The parties generally failed to inform the public of their legislative intentions on race and of the contents and objectives of specific race bills *before* their introduction in Parliament. An extreme example of this practice was Labour's handling of the 1968 Commonwealth Immigrants Act, which was presented, debated, and approved by both Houses of Parliament within a week. Although other legislation was debated more extensively in Parliament, only two acts—the 1965 Race Relations Act and the 1971 Immigration Act—were prefigured in the general-election manifesto of the governing party. Such practices reveal the reluctance of the parties to grapple with race-related issues before safely gaining office and their predilection to react to rather than anticipate events in this public policy area.

(iii) Racial buffering

The third strategy adopted by the parties to depoliticize race-related issues was to create and support what Katznelson has described as racial buffers (see Table 2.5). The National Committee for Commonwealth Immigrants (NCCI), the Community Relations Commission (CRCm), and the Commission for Racial Equality (CRE) have in effect transferred the primary responsibility for addressing and investigating race-related problems away from parties and party government to quasi-governmental bureaucratic bodies.[77] These buffers have depoliticized race in two specific ways. They have shielded politicians from the political hazards of addressing race issues directly. Elected officials have intervened on behalf of non-white constituents only when specific individual grievances have been brought to their door and when it has been politically advantageous to do so. By engaging in selective casework, they have appeared sympathetic to the problems of the non-white community without becoming actively involved in the larger conflicts plaguing

---

[77] Katznelson, op. cit., p. 180.

TABLE 2.5. *Creation of racial buffers, 1965–1977*

Organization	Origins
(1) National Committee for Commonwealth Immigrants (1965–8)	(1) Established by 1965 Labour White Paper, 'Immigration from the Commonwealth'
(2) Race Relations Board (1965–76)	(2) Established by 1965 Race Relations Act
(3) Community Relations Commission (1968–76)	(3) Established by 1968 Race Relations Act
(4) Commission for Racial Equality (1977–present)	(4) Established by 1976 Race Relations Act

their constituencies and, more importantly, without antagonizing whites.[78] National buffering institutions also have depoliticized race by inhibiting non-white political participation. By 'bureaucratizing' race-related issues, by divorcing non-white concerns from the political parties and mainstream politics, these institutions until recently acted as a political road-block for non-whites rather than a bridge between the non-white community and the government.[79] Although only partially successful in this purpose, these institutions unquestionably distracted the non-white community from focusing its attention and energies on party politics for the better part of a decade.[80]

All of these bodies were created by Labour governments and each was eventually superseded by another institution until 1977, when the Commission for Racial Equality was given the dual responsibility for both enforcing the Race Relations Acts and 'promoting' harmonious race relations, functions which will be examined in greater detail in Chapter 3. Despite the Conservatives' lack of initiative in this area, however, support for racial buffers—once they had been

[78] See e.g. 'Where is Labour's Race Policy?', *Tribune*, 16 June 1978.
[79] See Katznelson, op. cit., p. 177.
[80] Ibid.

created—was bipartisan. In addition to the Heath government's continued funding of these organizations and the
acquiescence of Conservative leaders in their creation, Conservative policy-makers, as we will see in Chapter 6,
informally approved their *raison d'être*. Indeed, for most of the
1960s and 1970s Conservative politicians often pointed to
their support of these bodies as evidence of their good
intentions toward settled immigrants. Both major parties used
the existence of these organizations for propaganda purposes
among non-whites and progressive white voters.[81]

How successful were the above strategies in taking race out
of British politics? In their more modest effort to extricate race
from the arena of party competition, the major parties
accomplished their purpose. After Smethwick threatened to
propel race to the national limelight, the issue did not emerge
as a major partisan concern between 1964 and 1975. In
particular, Labour's adoption of the views of its political
opposition yielded tangible results. Less than three years after
Labour's passionate opposition to the Conservative government's entry restrictions, 41 per cent of the electorate
perceived no difference between the major parties on
immigration, followed by 53 per cent indicating the absence of
party differences in this area in the spring of 1966.[82] When
voters who erroneously linked the views of Enoch Powell with
those of the Conservative leadership are excluded, it is quite
evident that most of the electorate saw few significant
differences between the major parties on race-related issues.
The successful avoidance by the parties of further Smethwicks
during this period and Labour's recapture of this troublesome
constituency in 1966 further prevented race becoming a
partisan issue.[83]

The success of the major parties in neutralizing race as a
partisan electoral issue did not extend, however, to their more
important attempts to remove race from the public agenda.

[81] Katznelson, op. cit., p. 180.

[82] As cited in, Donley T. Studlar, 'Policy Voting in Britain: The Coloured
Immigration Issue in the 1964, 1966, and 1970 General Elections', *American Political
Science Review*, 72.1, Mar. 1978, 46–64.

[83] See David Butler and Anthony King, *The British General Election of 1966*, New
York, St Martin's, 1966.

Despite the persistence of the major parties in skirting the subject, the enactment of ill-considered and contradictory legislation, and their continued support for racial buffers, the intensity of public sentiment on the issue and the level of citizen dissatisfaction with the relative silence of the parties did not diminish. As Table 2.6 clearly illustrates, almost two decades after the initial efforts of the Conservative and Labour parties to extricate the subject from political consideration, race-related issues remained politically salient and a potential source of partisan conflict.

TABLE 2.6. *Public awareness of race issues, 1978–1987*
(*% of respondents*)

(1) Feb. 1978: *Do you think on the whole this country has benefited or been harmed through immigrants coming to settle here from the Commonwealth?*

Benefited	Harmed	No difference	Don't know
20	45	23	12

(2) Oct. 1978: *Do you think a referendum should or should not be held to find out the voters' views about the number of immigrants coming to the country?*

Should	Should not	Don't know
74	19	7

(3) *Are the political parties saying too much about immigration, not saying enough, or the right amount is being said?*

		Too much	Not enough	About right	Don't know
Sept.	1978	21	48	20	11
Apr.	1980	17	47	25	11
Aug.	1981	18	49	22	11
Apr.	1982	13	47	25	15

(4) *In general, do you approve or disapprove of the way the government is handling immigration?*

		Approve	Disapprove	Don't know
Oct.	1978	26	59	15
Oct.	1979	46	37	17
Sept.	1980	31	44	25
June	1981	39	46	15
Sept.	1982	35	47	18
Oct.	1983	34	45	21
Feb.	1984	36	46	18
Oct.	1985	27	54	19
May	1986	29	52	19
Feb.	1987	38	46	17

Sources: Gallup Political Index 1978–87, London, Social Surveys (Gallup Poll) Limited; E. H. Hastings and P. K. Hastings (eds.), *Index to International Public Opinion, 1978–79*, Westport, Greenwood, 1980, p. 171; George H. Gallup (ed.), *The International Gallup Polls, Public Opinion 1978*, Wilmington, DE, Scholarly Resources Inc., 1980, p. 309.

MAINTAINING INTRA-PARTY DISCIPLINE

The political effects of the failure of the parties to depoliticize race will be examined in Chapter 5; among the most important of these consequences was the emergence of two extra-party movements concerned with race, the Anti-Nazi League and the National Front. Here, however, a more immediate consideration arises: how did Conservative and Labour leaders reconcile their intra-party differences? Specifically, how did party leaders successfully avert political infighting over race for more than a decade?

One factor working in favour of intra-party harmony was the hierarchical and centralized character of the Conservative and Labour parties, which gave their leaders the prerogative to impose a measure of party discipline on race-related subjects. This capability served the leadership well in initially formulating and then implementing the terms of their broader post-war consensus. One need only contrast British parties with their American and Italian counterparts, for instance, to appreciate how highly centralized they are. As McKenzie has documented, not only are British parties centre-orientated but they are, moreover, centre-directed.[84] In this respect, there were, until very recently, few significant differences between the major parties.

The pliability of the constituency associations of the parties virtually guaranteed that once the leadership had arrived at a political 'solution' on race, the whole of the party would accept the direction of the centre. The ability of Edward Heath to discharge Powell from the shadow cabinet, despite the latter's popularity and without precipitating a parliamentary or grass-roots revolt, demonstrated the political authority of the Conservative leader in enforcing the bipartisan racial consensus.[85] Similarly, Harold Wilson's pivotal role in effecting his party's about-face on immigration policy within a year of his ascent to the leadership indicated how receptive Labour was, in spite of its divisions, to a strong lead on race policy from the centre. The success of the party leaders in maintaining intra-party harmony did not endure indefinitely, nor was it invulnerable to either external or internal challenges. However, on the whole, intra-party unity on race prevailed between 1964 and 1975 in part as a consequence of the ability of party leaders to command respect for their policy decisions.

The success of the bipartisan consensus also derived from the dearth of organization among anti-consensus forces within and outside each party. A lack of cohesion was especially conspicuous outside Parliament, where constituency activists and party members opposed to the posture of their leaders were ineffective in voicing their opposition. The absence of a coherent opposition undoubtedly had multiple causes. However, at least two stand out as critical. First, the reluctance of activists and voters to engage in extra-parliamentary political activity essentially excluded this option as a form of protest. This was especially so among non-whites who, according to Freeman, were 'denied prominent spokesmen from among the leadership of the major parties and . . . [were] hampered in

[84] R. T. McKenzie, *British Political Parties*, London, Praeger, 1963, p. ix.
[85] For a brief discussion of this point see Butler and Pinto-Duschinsky, op. cit., pp. 78–80.

organizing into a political force'.[86] Although Conservative
activists supported local anti-immigrant groups and Labour-
ites supported progressive organizations such as the Campaign Against Racial Discrimination (CARD), such groups
were often short-lived.[87] When party leaders resisted such
pressures, most of these groups splintered into warring
factions, thus further diminishing their potential influence.
Moreover, even when the opponents of the consensus were
well organized, their effectiveness was often undermined by
the ability of Conservative and Labour leaders to manipulate
them. This was usually accomplished by appropriating the
demands of these groups in a manner which preserved the
racial consensus. Labour leaders were particularly adept at
such manœuvering. For example, they incorporated the advice
and taxed the energies of CARD during the formulation of the
1965 Race Relations Act, while ensuring that such legislation
presented few insurmountable barriers to the practice of racial
discrimination, CARD's central concern. As Rose *et al.*
described the outcome of Labour's successful appropriation of
CARD's fragile coalition:

These [dissimilar] groups had temporarily come together in
coalition under the twin pressures of dissatisfaction with the
capacity of the existing organizations to provide a satisfactory lead
on external wants, and the internal race-relations situation; the
emphasis on further legislation had provided for a time the
necessarily common aim. With the achievement, leaving only the far
less glamorous task of ensuring that the form of legislation was
satisfactory, . . . the coalition fell apart.[88]

Conservative leaders too kept critics of the racial consensus off
balance, verbally adopting a hard line on non-white immigration to placate the right wing of the party, while allowing
substantial numbers of immigrants to enter Britain under
categories not covered by the Conservatives' own immigration

---

[86] Freeman op. cit., p. 128.
[87] See Benjamin W. Heineman Jr., *The Politics of the Powerless*, London, IRR/OUP,
1972.
[88] E. J. B. Rose and Associates, *Colour and Citizenship*, London, IRR/OUP, 1969,
p. 543.

restrictions, categories which the major parties had implicitly agreed to leave outside the scope of legislation.

Why did the architects of Butskellism, and principally Hugh Gaitskell, allow race to become a partisan issue in the first place? Specifically, why did Gaitskell vigorously oppose immigration controls, thus politicizing the issue? In addressing ourselves to this question, the context in which the race issue arose must be considered. As we have seen, until the political earthquake in Smethwick there was no reason to suspect that race would become politically prominent. Neither Gaitskell nor the Conservative leadership foresaw, before 1961, the extent to which race would galvanize public opinion. Neither major party had sufficient reason to suppress the issue and, apart from the feeble efforts of Conservative leaders to placate the right wing of the party by introducing entry controls, neither party gave the issue more than cursory consideration.[89] Katznelson's report that the Macmillan government was 'utterly shocked' by Gaitskell's 1961 parliamentary address, 'by his indignation, by the force of his opposition' to restrictions, indicates how politically inconsequential Conservative leaders believed the immigration question was.

With the advent of Smethwick all of this changed. From relative obscurity the race issue suddenly assumed a high political profile with the Wilson government particularly anxious to discover a political solution to the problem. As we have seen, the manner in which the major parties addressed race after 1964—by depoliticizing the subject—was self-serving, leaving both the electorate and party activists discontented in the long term (see Chapters 5 and 6). In the short term, however, Conservative and Labour leaders

[89] Jim Bulpitt, 'Continuity, Autonomy and Peripheralization: The Autonomy of the Centre's Race Statecraft in England', in Z. Layton-Henry and P. B. Rich (eds.), *Race, Government and Politics in Britain*, London, Macmillan, 1986, p. 27.

effectively created a political breathing space in which further Smethwicks were avoided and race was relegated to the periphery of British politics. Enoch Powell excepted, the leaders of both major parties successfully imposed their bipartisan approach to the issue on the whole of their respective organizations. Through a mixture of persuasion and political manipulation Conservative and Labour leaders preserved intra-party discipline in this policy area for over a decade.

3

Depoliticizing Race Locally:
The Role of Community Relations Councils

INTRODUCTION

While immigration restrictions and the suppression of debate by the major political parties partially depoliticized the race issue nationally, these strategies were clearly inadequate to manage local race-related difficulties. Indeed, it could be argued that because national political élites were insulated from grass-roots pressures on race, race-related conflict locally was exacerbated.[1] Thus, in many localities the major parties attempted to extricate race from politics by supporting welfare-orientated organizations known as Voluntary Liaison Committees (VLCs), later called Community Relations Councils (CRCs).[2] As local administrative structures dealing with race relations, Community Relations Councils are uniquely British. Neither France nor West Germany, for instance, with their similar post-war immigration patterns, nor the United States with its large, mobile, black population, invented an equivalent of the local British CRC. How CRCs emerged and became entrenched as the dominant organization in local British race relations will be explored in this chapter.

Many of the data contained in this chapter were supplied by CRCs. Of the 97 local committees which were contacted by either phone or post, 40 agreed to participate in our study, including 13 which were visited by the author and 27 which

---

[1] Jim Bulpitt, 'Continuity, Autonomy and Peripheralization: The Autonomy of the Centre's Race Statecraft in England', in, Z. Layton-Henry and P. B. Rich (eds.), *Race, Government and Politics in Britain*, London, Macmillan, 1986, pp. 17–44.
[2] Included under the label CRC are all local race committees and organizations known as 'councils for racial equality', 'committees for community relations' and other similar names.

responded to a written questionnaire.[3] The size, variety, and geographic distribution of our sample suggest its representativeness.

Community Relations Councils, or Voluntary Liaison Committees as they were known between 1965 and 1968, spontaneously emerged as independent local organizations with few ties to national agencies.[4] For the most part, community leaders and a motley group of civic-minded residents came together in the various localities to assist arriving immigrants. Numerous international friendship societies, committees for the welfare of immigrants, and other similarly named organizations were founded between 1955 and 1964 in areas of non-white immigrant settlement. Most available evidence indicates that these bodies were intended only to be temporary assistance centres.[5]

In a favourable political environment, however, the community relations movement grew quickly. From 15 com-

[3] The Commission for Racial Equality in November 1980 officially recognized 101 committees. Thus, the 97 CRCs which were contacted in 1980 and 1981 represented almost the complete universe of CRCs. The 40 in our sample included 14 CRCs located in Greater London, 5 in south-west England, 6 in south-east England, 5 in the Midlands, 3 in north-west England, 5 in Yorkshire and north-west England, and 2 in Scotland.

[4] It has been argued that the National Committee for Commonwealth Immigrants, through its offer of modest financial assistance, was responsible for the formation of many new race committees. The fact that many contemporary committees emerged during the NCCI's tenure between 1965 and 1968 is commonly cited as evidence supporting this claim. Yet, it is incorrect to conclude from this that the emergence of most CRCs was due to NCCI support. In our sample, for instance, over half of the 20 CRCs that were established between 1965 and 1968 reported that it was not until years after they were founded that the NCCI, and its successor, the Community Relations Commission, extended recognition. One CRC was in existence for ten years before a full-time CRO was appointed. These CRCs were propped up at an early juncture by voluntary labour, charitable contributions and, in some instances, small grants by local authorities. In fact, many CRCs which emerged between 1965 and 1970 (and certainly those which were established before the birth of the NCCI in 1965) had little or no national support. The NCCI reinforced what began as a local, spontaneous initiative.

[5] E. J. B. Rose and Associates, *Colour and Citizenship*, London, IRR/OUP, 1969, pp. 382–3.

mittees founded by 1964, the number of CRCs rose to 42 in 1966, 50 in 1967, 78 in 1969, and over 100 local committees recognized by the Commission for Racial Equality in 1988. These numbers, moreover, under-represent the complete CRC universe. Precise figures are not available, but the collapse of several CRCs, for financial and other reasons, means that few areas in England have not had some experience of a Community Relations Council.

More impressive than the size of the CRC movement is its breadth. Although a quarter of all CRCs are located in Greater London, the remaining 75 per cent are scattered throughout Great Britain, including several in Wales and a handful in Scotland. Predictably, most CRCs can be found in areas of ethnic-minority concentration. In the South-East Region (encompassing Greater London), where more than 4 per cent of the population is estimated to be of New Commonwealth and Pakistani origin, there are over 35 CRCs. In the West and East Midlands there are 21 CRCs. With two exceptions, all London boroughs with an estimated New Commonwealth-born population of 20,000 or more have a CRC. Community Relations Councils have also been founded in Birmingham, Bradford, Coventry, Leicester, Manchester, and Wolverhampton.

As organizations preoccupied with 'harmonizing' community relations, Community Relations Councils were promising pawns in the strategy of the Conservative and Labour parties to extricate race from politics and, as a consequence, received bipartisan support during the heyday of the racial consensus. The use of Community Relations Councils to depoliticize race at the local level is illustrated by the early example of Nottingham. Race became a highly charged political issue in Nottingham after a series of violent disturbances which rocked the city and the country in 1958. Before these disturbances, the Nottingham VLC had requested the assistance of its local authority in appointing a special welfare worker, and permission to use the city's information centre for weekly advice sessions. The local authority initially refused on the grounds that it 'would not be proper to appoint a Welfare Officer for one small group, nor would it be proper to provide any services above those available for citizens as a whole'.[6] Within a year after the riots, however, the local Council authorized a £500 annual grant to the VLC, and an additional £500 loan to the Coloured Peoples Housing Association. The Nottingham Council also appointed an education worker with special responsibility for the non-white community. The Nottingham disturbances undoubtedly served as a warning and motivated the major political parties in other areas with sizeable non-white populations to support voluntary committees.[7]

Although the first CRCs usually enjoyed bipartisan sponsorship, it soon became obvious that Labour was more strongly committed to CRCs than the Conservative party. Labour's close ties to the CRC movement, and in particular the prominent role played by Labour activists in founding many local committees, have been extensively documented. It is well known that CRCs share many of Labour's positions on race-related issues (e.g. the party's advocacy of legislation to combat racial discrimination), although numerous committees have criticized the record of Labour governments on immigration. Officials at the Commission for Racial Equality have admitted privately that most community relations officers (CROs) are Labour sympathizers.[8]

In addition to these explicit connections, there is evidence that Labour authorities are more sympathetic to the work of CRCs. Of the 30 CRCs in our sample who had had experience of both Conservative and Labour-majority Councils, 12 reported better relations with Labour; the remaining 18 saw little or no difference between the parties. Not one CRC reported a closer relationship with the Conservatives. As several CROs reported:

The Tories loathe us and I have no doubt they will attempt to withdraw our funding if and when they're returned to power. They've tried this (unsuccessfully) in the past.

We receive more cooperation . . . under Labour and no-majority Councils.

The CRC . . . has worked better with the Labour Council because

[6] Ira Katznelson, *Black Men, White Cities*, London, OUP, 1973, p. 159.
[7] Ibid.
[8] Author's interviews with CRE officials.

many of the Labour councillors have been long serving members of the . . . CRC and its predecessors.

Our relationship with the Labour Council is always better than with the Conservatives.

The Conservative Council actively blocked the appointment of a CRO. Labour set it up as soon as they were in power.

Our relationship with the Tory Council is not as close as it was with Labour. I had a working relationship with the Labour Council that ceased to exist when the Tories came in.

According to the National Association of Community Relations Councils, a Labour Council has never refused to support an existing committee. In theory, CRCs are non-partisan organizations, but many committees continue to survive as a result of their close relationship with local Labour politicians. Most community relations officers prefer to see the Labour party control the Town Hall.[9]

Why should Labour be more supportive of CRCs if both major parties benefited from the racial consensus? Labour has historically had a greater stake in preserving the consensus. Throughout the 1960s and 1970s Labour was faced with more severe electoral cross-pressures over race than the Conservative party. Labour's short-term electoral success and long-term viability as a party depended upon substantial working-class support. On the one hand, such support included most of Britain's non-white voters who, according to the Community Relations Commission, 'swung the election' for the Labour party in both 1974 general elections.[10] On the other hand, anti-immigrant sentiment was and remains pervasive among the white working class, especially in Labour's electoral strongholds in declining industrial areas. By supporting CRCs the party nationally and locally could appear to aid ethnic minorities without overtly offending racially prejudiced whites.

The Conservative party also supported CRCs for political reasons; it adhered to this course, however, only as long as it also was politically cross-pressured. These pressures, as we

---

[9] Author's interviews with community relations officers.
[10] *The Participation of the Ethnic Minorities in the General Election, October, 1974*, London, CRCm, Community Relations Commissions 1975.

saw in Chapter 2, derived from the conflict among factions within the party which sought to preserve the Commonwealth, those who wished to maintain the flow of immigrant labour, and proponents of immigration restrictions. The attitudes of the major parties toward CRCs partially diverged in the 1970s because of the *decreasing* political cross-pressures on the Conservative party, as advocates of racial buffers gradually disappeared from circles of party influence (see Chapter 6).

Until the mid-1970s, however, both parties pinned their local depoliticization strategy on Community Relations Councils. The successful transformation of CRCs into racial buffers was predicated on the assumptions that first, CRCs could be tied to government, made dependent upon its goodwill and financial support; and second, that this political association would enable the parties to manipulate the local committees. Central to this strategy was the belief that CRCs could and would attract most of the local community's influential non-whites and engage them in apolitical activities which would effectively neutralize if not exhaust their political energy. At the same time, and despite the participation of non-whites in CRCs, the parties calculated they could prevent these organizations from evolving into a platform for non-white protest.

In order for the expectations of the parties to be realized, however, the structure, financing, and membership of CRCs, and their relationships with local and national government had to be altered. Although the local committees were to retain their essential identity, CRCs had to be made accountable to political authorities. To achieve this, the parties incorporated CRCs into a national race-relations administrative structure.

THE CENTRAL CO-ORDINATION OF CRCS

The first national agency to 'co-ordinate' the local committees was the National Committee for Commonwealth Immigrants (NCCI), which evolved from the Labour government's 1965 White Paper 'Immigration from the Commonwealth'. The

NCCI was instructed by the government's White Paper to 'promote . . . the activities of Voluntary Liaison Committees and advise them on their work' and, where necessary, assist 'in the recruitment and training of suitable men and women to serve on these committees as full-time officials'.[11] The NCCI in effect 'promoted' the activities of the Voluntary Liaison Committees by funding the salaries of full-time liaison officers (CROs) who headed the local committees. During its first year of existence the NCCI allocated £1,500 each to 32 VLCs.

How well did the NCCI fulfil its White Paper directives? In retrospect, two things are clear: first, the NCCI compromised the autonomy of the local committees by subjecting them to specific requirements, such as the rule that the governing constitutions of the VLCs had to conform to an NCCI model; and second, despite these constraints, most VLCs were only loosely associated with the NCCI between 1965 and 1968. The National Committee was given neither sufficient resources nor manpower to co-ordinate VLC activities.

Grants from the NCCI, however, permitted CRCs to appoint full-time community relations officers, thus establishing CRCs as semi-permanent, quasi-official institutions. It accomplished this in two ways. The central funding of CRO salaries allowed the local committees to survive their original founders. It detached the committees from the local community, as CRCs came to depend less on charitable contributions and voluntary labour. Moreover, centralized CRO funding gave the committees an official status that was denied other, often more politically militant, local race groups. Lack of official recognition did not necessarily discredit other groups, but it did encourage local authorities to support CRCs exclusively, further bolstering their position in the community. Other agencies, in and out of government, soon followed suit until CRCs became universally recognized as the principal race organization at the local level.

Association with the NCCI also tied VLCs financially to the National Committee, effecting subtle changes in their character. The funding of officer salaries by the NCCI

<hr />

[11] *Immigration from the Commonwealth*, Cmnd. 2739, London, HMSO, Aug. 1965.

encouraged VLCs to employ full-time race relations 'professionals'. With national funding, the local committees slowly evolved into semi-permanent administrative structures with a potentially unlimited future. Moreover, a sense of 'establishment' encouraged VLC workers to take the 'high road' on race by concentrating almost exclusively on activities which promised to preserve 'racial harmony' rather than raise unsettling questions about ethnic-minority disadvantage in British society.

The replacement of the NCCI with the Community Relations Commission (CRCm) in 1968 further reinforced the official status of CRCs. The Commission, unlike its predecessor, was a statutory body which evolved from section 25 of the 1968 Race Relations Act. The Commission was empowered under the Act to 'give financial assistance to any local organizations appearing to the Commission to be concerned with community relations'.[12] Toward this end, the government granted CRCm £200,000 during its first full year.

From its founding, the Commission was preoccupied with managing CRCs. In 1970, for example, the Commission circulated a working paper which proposed four alternatives to the then loose CRC–CRCm association. The options offered to community relations officers were: employment of community relations officers by local government; creation of a regional CRC structure with CROs employed on a regional basis; direct hiring of CROs by the Commission; and maintaining the existing CRC–CRCm relationship with unspecified changes. The introduction of these proposals by the Commission, according to Mullard, was primarily intended to raise the subject of CRO employment, given the preference of the CRCm for centralized CRO employment.[13] To justify its preference the Commission cited the 'greater degree of professionalism; increased job mobility for officers; job training opportunities; and the uniformity of CRO conditions of service' which would result from centralized officer employment.[14] Most CROs were not persuaded by

[12] *Race Relations Act*, ch. 71, London, HMSO, 1968.
[13] Chris Mullard, *Black Britain*, London, Allen and Unwin, 1973, pp. 112–16.
[14] Ibid., p. 113.

these arguments. CROs vigorously resisted the Commission's proposals and maintained their local employment.

The attempts by the Commission to impose a central administrative structure on the community-relations movement created serious tensions between the CRCm and the local committees. Longer-established CRCs were especially hostile toward the Commission's proposals, which they perceived as a threat to their independence. Moreover, the ambitions of the Commission were not the only cause of friction. As Charles Boxer, a former CRO, describes the conflict:

It was always beyond the CRCm's ability to lay down and enforce priorities. Not only was it difficult for the CRCm to act thus because of the independence of CRCs but the inability of the CRCm to understand the motivation of CRCs . . . made any such programme of priorities inappropriate and inadequate and therefore unworkable. There was also a tendency in the CRCm to develop an élitist view of CRCs. Once people were employed by the CRCm they were thought to be more expert, more knowledgeable and the views of CRCs less credible.[15]

To many, if not most, CRCs the CRCm was the 'enemy' working on behalf of the central government to divorce race relations work from local control. Between 1968 and 1977 relations between the two sides were often openly antagonistic.

Friction between the CRCm and the local committees did little to retard the growing financial dependence of CRCs on the Commission, however. By 1977 virtually every local committee in the country was receiving grants from the CRCm for CRO salaries, and many applied for and received funds for special projects. Indeed, despite failing to centralize the employment of CROs, the Commission succeeded in asserting greater central control over the local committees than its predecessor. At the end of its tenure the CRCm could claim that virtually all CRCs were operating within basic Commission guide-lines.[16]

---

[15] Charles Boxer, 'CRCs and the CRE', unpublished paper, 1977.
[16] These guide-lines included the requirement that CRCs receive political support and funding from their local authority and the recommendation that the police be affiliated to the local committees.

The Commission for Racial Equality (CRE), which superseded the Community Relations Commission in August 1977,
sought further control over CRCs. Soon after assuming office
the new Commission reopened the subject of CRO employment with the publication of a Green Paper which proposed
six models from which CROs could choose to base their future
relationship with the Commission.[17] At least three of these
were hardly attractive options to most CROs since each would
have eventually abolished the local committees. Another two,
only slightly more palatable choices, would have divorced
CROs from their local committees. Confronted with these
alternatives, over two-thirds of all CROs acceded to the Commission's final option to reform the CRE–CRC relationship.

Among the changes being implemented by the CRE are
'agreed policy and priority plans', a reform which effectively
subjects the work of CRCs to the approval of the CRE.
Designating these plans 'work programmes', the Commission
has vaguely articulated their nature and purpose:

They will be collaborative exercises to establish the framework of co-
operation between the . . . [CRE and CRCs]. In short, CRCs will be
responsible for the drawing up and administration of the work
programmes. The Commission will provide professional support as
and when necessary. Work programmes will be of three to five years'
duration and will be subject to annual review between the CRE and
CRCs. The Commission would wish to assist in the preparation of
programmes and in any modification to them during their
implementation.[18]

The Commission, as the above language makes clear, remains
interested in its predecessors' aim of managing CRCs.
Moreover, under the vague conditions it has established for
the withdrawal of CRC grant aid the Commission is well
placed to see that its reforms are implemented. To date, the
CRE has not been unwilling to resort to financial pressure in
dealing with rebellious committees.[19]

[17] Commission for Racial Equality, *The Nature and Structure of Local Work for Racial Equality*, London, CRE, 1978.
[18] Commission for Racial Equality, *The Nature and Funding of Local Race Relations Work*, London, CRE, 1980, p. 8.
[19] The case of Wolverhampton CRC is illustrative. It is discussed in Barking and Dagenham Council for Racial Equality, *Annual Report 1980*, p. 7; Walsall Council for Community Relations, *Annual Report 1979/1980*, p. 17; and National Association of

CRCS AND THEIR LOCAL AUTHORITIES

The most direct influence on the work and orientation of CRCs is their local authority. The political parties effectively discipline CRCs through the selective use of financial incentives and penalties by local government.

The CRC–local government relationship has been inherently conflictual. On the one hand, CRCs depend on the Town Hall for financial assistance, information, and political support. As many of the CROs we interviewed observed, racial disadvantage cannot be combatted successfully without the co-operation of the local authority. Yet many of the race-related problems that CRCs attempt to rectify spring from the apathy, negligence, or racism of local authorities. If local authorities fulfilled their statutory obligations in housing, employment, and education, CRCs would have decidedly less reason for existing.

Section 71 of the 1976 Race Relations Act ostensibly establishes a link between the work of CRCs and the responsibility of local authorities to discourage racial discrimination. The Act states:

It shall be the duty of every local authority to make appropriate arrangements with the view to securing that their various functions are carried out with due regard to the need (a) to eliminate unlawful discrimination; and (b) to promote the equality of opportunity, and good race relations, between persons of different racial groups.[20]

Missing from the statute, however, are specific legal directives to local government. As a result, the overwhelming majority of authorities have done little to fulfil this obligation: according to one survey, only six London boroughs took concrete steps through 1980 to fulfil their responsibilities as prescribed by section 71.[21] In this context, some local authorities offer their financial support of CRCs as evidence that they are complying

Community Relations Councils, 'Proposals for Establishing a Working Relationship Between the National Association of Community Relations Councils and the Commission for Racial Equality', London, 1980.

[20] *Race Relations Act*, ch. 74, London, HMSO, 1976, p. 47.
[21] Trevor Phillips, *Skin Programme*, London Weekend Television, 9 Nov. 1980. More recent surveys indicate greater progress. See Usha Prashar and Shan Nicholas, *Routes or Roadblocks?*, London, Runnymede Trust, 1986.

with their duties under the 1976 Race Relations Act. These committees are often well funded; many automatically receive inflation-adjusted increases in their annual local authority grant.

Whether modest or ample, local-authority financial assistance has sustained most committees. Almost half of our sample receive 51 per cent or more of their total revenues from local government, including 11 CRCs which are completely dependent upon local-authority funds. For most committees local-authority funds cover administrative overhead costs, and, in larger CRCs, fund staff other than the CRO. Local authority financing thus enables CRCs to meet primary expenses.

These figures, moreover, understate the dependence of CRCs on their local authorities. In addition to their own grants, local authorities indirectly influence other sources of CRC funding. For example, in order to receive CRE funding and recognition a prospective CRC must secure at least a modest local-authority grant. The CRE is wary of aiding existing committees and will rarely recognize new ones which do not enjoy the confidence of their local authority. Furthermore, in order for CRCs to be awarded Urban Aid funds from central government, local authorities must match 25 per cent of the total amount of these grants. Without an initial local-authority grant a prospective CRC is unlikely to get off the ground. Without continued local-authority financial support an established committee is unlikely to remain viable.

As many CRCs have discovered, local-authority support is not automatic. Where local committees have disappointed the expectations of their local authorities by engaging in 'political' or other prohibited activities, local authorities have quickly eliminated CRC funding. The following excerpts from a letter written by the leader of a London borough Council to his CRC chairman demonstrate the pressure that local authorities can exert:

I feel it is only right to draw to your attention that I and a number of my colleagues have received representations over a considerable period concerning the way your organization operates which we and the complainants consider is not wholly satisfactory. . . . I am afraid your organization cannot expect the same level of support from the

Council [in the next financial year] . . . and we will be even more critical in ensuring that all our money is being well spent.[22]

How does a local authority determine that its money is being well spent? Specifically, what is expected of CRCs, and what is forbidden? Most local authorities expect CRCs to concentrate on social welfare projects. Beyond this, monitoring racial discrimination in the local community is tolerated, partially because such activity is advocated by the CRE, but primarily because there is little conflict between this function and the broader role envisioned. However, monitoring discriminatory practices in local government and political lobbying are considered by local authorities to be inappropriate CRC activities.

Below, we examine the three roles which CRCs have historically adopted: that of social welfare agencies, legal watchdogs, and campaigning bodies. We see that although the policy options of CRCs are constrained by political pressures, the proximity of CRCs to the roots of racial disadvantage often impel them to act against rather than in concert with their political sponsors.

(i) CRCs as social welfare agencies

Virtually all of the early Voluntary Liaison Committees were preoccupied with providing welfare assistance to non-white immigrants. Most often, such assistance involved advising individuals on immigration and citizenship matters, helping to fight court cases, establishing housing associations, organizing children's playgroups, and other related activities. By 1969, however, the authors of *Colour and Citizenship* reported that social work was becoming less important within the community-relations movement; in their study of CRCs two years later Hill and Issacharoff confirmed this finding and argued that 'some committees are so concerned to avoid becoming casework agencies . . . that they are not prepared to tackle this kind of work'.[23]

[22] Letter written by Councillor J. I. Wood to Ealing borough CRC Chairman, Cedric Mastin, 1 Dec. 1980.
[23] See Rose, op. cit., p. 388; and M. J. Hill and R. M. Issacharoff, *Community Action and Race Relations*, London, IRR/OUP, 1971, p. 175.

Contrary to these earlier reports, however, our research discovered that social work remains a high local committee priority. When asked whether their committees performed this role, nearly three-fifths of the CROs participating in our survey answered affirmatively. Moreover, our written responses actually understate the extent to which contemporary CRCs are orientated toward social work. An examination of CRC annual reports and other documents revealed that many more committees engaged in welfare-related activities than were reported in our written questionnaires. In addition to the 59 per cent of CRCs that identified with a social service role, another 38 per cent could be seen to perform this function. With only one exception, all the CRCs for whom we had data engaged in some form of social work, from operating pre-school day nurseries to running short-stay hostels for homeless youth.

Evidence of these activities does not necessarily refute the argument, of course, that CRCs are gradually moving away from social work. What does is the enthusiasm many CRCs continue to demonstrate for these activities:

Casework is one of the most important functions of the CRC. Our amount of casework is unlimited, but to carry out efficient casework we need more staff and resources. With our few resources and only one full time staff member, we have nevertheless dealt with many cases and with hundreds of telephone enquiries.

Playschemes, adventure playgrounds, home tutor schemes and English language classes perhaps seem different from demonstrations and campaigns but the local CRC see these as important parts of our work.

Individual problems in the community have been dealt with on a casework basis covering different aspects, e.g. housing, social services, neighbourhood disputes, matrimonial disputes, and other problems. Assistance has been rendered where an interpreter was needed.

The amount of casework we dealt with this year was more than ten times greater than last year.

There was a 50 per cent increase in cases and enquiries. These were individuals visiting the office during the first half of the year, totalling 2,060.

Fifty per cent of our total work involves casework. This entails all cases which other agencies cannot cater for because of a lack of specialist knowledge.

Indeed, most CRCs will continue to invest considerable time and resources in welfare-related activities for several reasons. First, and most importantly, local authorities encourage the welfare role. As the conflicts between CRCs and local authorities in Ealing, Redbridge, and other areas have demonstrated, CRCs that neglect or de-emphasize their welfare function are likely to antagonize their local authority.[24] Second, CRC employees usually come from social-work backgrounds, including many with previous social work training and experience. These people are likely to continue to concentrate on welfare-related activities. Finally, many local committees, as registered charities, risk losing their tax-exempt status if they do not act as charities. Financial considerations thus require that social services be maintained and publicly promoted.

(ii) CRCs as legal watchdogs

The practice of Community Relations Councils acting as legal watchdogs, monitoring the compliance of local employers and other organizations with anti-discrimination statutes, became prevalent with the passage of the 1976 Race Relations Act. The Act replaced the Community Relations Commission with the Commission for Racial Equality and empowered the CRE to enforce its anti-discrimination clauses. Although the Statute did not refer specifically to CRCs as legal watchdogs, it nevertheless stimulated these oganizations to assume first the function of watchdog, because the CRE would need CRCs as local informants and allies to fulfil its legal mandate to eliminate racial discrimination locally; and second, the general enthusiasm engendered by the passage of the new Race Act among race relations workers encouraged many CRCs to believe they now had firm legal ground on which to stand in fighting discrimination. Moreover, the monitoring

---

[24] Both CRCs had been accused by their local authorities of being politically orientated. For a concise summary of Ealing CRC's difficulties see 'Grants are Axed', *New Equals*, 16 Apr. 1981.

function was perceived by the National Association of Community Relations Councils as a role for which CRCs were well suited.[25]

In practice, CRCs fulfil their watchdog duties in one of two ways. The first is through formal investigations, of which a study of job discrimination in the Nottingham area by the Nottingham District Community Relations Council is a well-publicized but atypical example.[26] The second, more frequent, means of monitoring violations of the Race Relations Acts is to establish subcommittees or panels to investigate specific allegations of racial discrimination. An examination of CRC annual reports revealed the investigation of discrimination through the establishment of panels to be a common CRC practice. At least 20 local committees, or two-thirds of those whose practices we could verify, had formed panels to monitor discrimination in community employment or had delegated this responsibility to a full-time, CRC employment officer. At the very least this evidence suggests that the local committees are serious about their role of legal watchdog in the employment field. .

One might also expect housing, education, and the provision of goods, facilities, and services (areas also covered under the 1976 Race Relations Act) to be prime target areas for CRC watchdog committees. Fifty-seven per cent of our London sample have established a housing committee: among these CRCs housing appears to be the second most adopted issue for a panel after employment. Yet, while most CRCs have created at least one subcommittee besides the one for employment, these panels differ from CRC employment panels in a key respect: instead of being legal watchdogs, their activities often resemble social work.

It has proved difficult for CRCs to monitor discrimination in fields other than employment for two reasons. Racial discrimination in local employment is, first of all, more easily monitored because the policies of a few large firms (where local committees concentrate their attention and efforts) affect many individuals. Unlike residential accommodation in the

---

[25] National Association of Community Relations Councils, 'Setting Objectives', London, 1979.

[26] Commission for Racial Equality, *Half a Chance?*, London, CRE, 1980.

private sector, which is normally sought out and provided on an individual basis, employment practices by private companies are continuous activities, affecting numerous workers. More significant, however, is the fact that the private sector, which has little leverage over CRCs, generates most local employment. Most social services on the other hand are provided by local government, which does exert influence over CRCs.

CRC watchdog committees monitor the policies of their local authorities to varying degrees. Some CRCs, especially within Greater London, aggressively challenge their local authorities in this spirit:

[We are] aware that the borough is in contravention of the Race Relations Act 1976 in perpetuating policies which result in a section of the community being at disadvantage. We have taken legal advice and may, in due course, be forced to take the Council to court. Meanwhile we continue our work in collecting and collating information to put before the Council.

We complained to the majority party on the Council that little action, if any, had been taken over a period of eight months to implement the equal opportunity policy. The result is that we were invited to spell out in detail what decisions need to be taken and then, together with staff union representatives, to join a monitoring group whose task it would be to ensure that these decisions were carried out.

But examples of CRCs challenging the policies of their local authority are few, consisting of a clear minority of all the local committees we examined. For obvious reasons, few authorities fund CRCs which criticize their policies, and CRCs which closely monitor the practices of local government do so at their peril. This is especially true where local governments contravene the spirit if not the letter of anti-discrimination statutes.

(iii) CRCs as campaigning bodies

The role of a public campaigning organization is one which CRCs have only recently and hesitatingly adopted. To avoid controversy all but a handful of the early Voluntary Liaison Committees shunned political activism, preferring to fight racism more discreetly. Most early CRCs yielded the lead in

anti-racist public education to national organizations like the
Campaign Against Racial Discrimination (CARD). Only
when groups like CARD disappeared in the late 1960s and
early 1970s did a significant number of local committees
embrace public campaigning. Although far less political than
CARD, these campaigning CRCs have tended nevertheless to
become embroiled in political controversy.

The primary objective of CRC campaigns is to bring issues
which disproportionately affect ethnic minorities to the
attention of the general public. Normally, this is accomplished
via the mass media:

If there is to be progress toward the implementation of policies for
racial equality, then there must be a radical shift in public opinion
and public attitudes. To achieve this requires public education and
propaganda. . . . [We seek] to support and foster initiatives and
campaigns in concert with ethnic-minority groups and progressive
organizations to combat the ideas associated with racism and
fascism. This [the CRC] seeks to do by the circulation and
publication of information through community initiatives and all
available channels of the media.

Although CRCs were slow to take up campaigning, most
CRCs currently view this as an important function. Fifty-six
per cent of the committees in our survey indicated that they
spent some time and resources, however exiguous, in
campaigning on particular issues. Interestingly, almost three-
quarters of these committees were founded before 1969. This
finding may indicate that local committees become more
politically orientated the longer they are established.

The reluctance of many CRCs to take up campaigning can
primarily be explained by the conflict local committees invite
with their local authority by engaging in this activity. Unlike
the provision of welfare services, single-issue campaigns can
embarrass local government. CRC campaigns concerned with
homelessness or residential overcrowding, for example, touch
upon local-authority responsibilities. As such, calling
attention to these issues can highlight local-government
shortcomings. Moreover, even national issues, such as
immigration and nationality questions, may have a local
dimension. This is particularly the case when the majority

parties of both the local Council and the national government are the same, creating a situation where an attack on the central government can be construed as a challenge to the local party. In these circumstances, it is hardly surprising that many CRCs avoid campaigning on single issues. To do so is to jeopardize their existence.

CRCS AND THE NON-WHITE COMMUNITY

The major political parties' support for CRCs, as we have seen, was predicated upon the ability of these organizations to attract prominent non-whites and non-white groups. By becoming involved in CRCs, it was hoped, non-whites would engage in apolitical activities and be discouraged from organizing politically. To achieve this, CRCs were to refrain from developing, as a logical extension of their association with ethnic minorities, into platforms for political protest. Has the strategy of the parties worked? Specifically, have CRCs attracted the expected non-white membership? Have CRCs avoided becoming a platform for non-white protest? Have CRCs successfully inhibited the development of alternative, non-white representative bodies?

To placate their local authorities CRCs have been motivated to present visible evidence that prominent non-whites are incorporated within their orbit. In this context, the exercise of gathering scores of 'affiliations', especially from ethnic-minority community groups, creates the appearance that CRCs are performing the role expected of them. From the perspective of local authorities, this CRC practice is attractive for two reasons: first, by concentrating on groups and not individual affiliates CRCs are reaching only the already organized; non-whites outside this group world and, specifically, those outside the political arena remain unorganized. This practice has the obvious advantage, for local authorities, of decreasing the chances that a hitherto unpoliticized segment of the ethnic-minority community will become politically active as a consequence of their affiliation with the local committees. Second, the group affiliation structure has the effect, perhaps intended, of making CRCs less democratic and, hence, less open to groups challenging their conservative orientation.[27]

Community Relations Councils have gathered these group affiliations zealously; most local committees can boast that 50 to 150 organizations are included in their membership. However, in most instances, these are merely paper affiliations. In reality, ethnic-minority leaders have exercised little if any influence over the daily management of CRCs. Many of the largest CRCs throughout the country are effectively controlled by white, albeit well-intentioned, community-relations officers and white-dominated executive committees. CRCs in this respect have not evolved into the racial buffers the political parties had hoped they would. But neither have CRCs evolved into the non-white representative organizations that some local authorities feared they might. However, many CRCs have become active ethnic-minority pressure groups. To the vexation of local authorities, it is upon them that these pressures are often applied.

Concern about substandard housing conditions, educational disadvantage, poor health care, and other community problems disproportionately affecting non-whites motivated a number of the first Voluntary Liaison Committees to lobby the Town Hall for remedial policies. Perceiving that little could be accomplished, even in the area of social welfare, without local authority co-operation, these VLCs forged links with local government civil servants, elected councillors, and other officials. By the late 1970s, however, CRCs became more amenable to adopting the role of a gadfly in their relations with local government. In 1979 the National Association of Community Relations Councils urged CRCs to work toward the 'inclusion of [the] "racial dimension" as a regular item on major [local government] committees, thus ensuring continuing assessment of relevance of policies to ethnic minorities'.[28] While the recommendation of the

---

[27] Hill and Issacharoff imply that the NCCI's recommendation that CRCs be primarily 'organizations of organizations' was intended to maintain their conservative orientation, op. cit., pp. 81–97. The CRE has continued this policy. As a condition of grant-aid to CRCs, the Commission has expressed its preference that individual members comprise no more than one-quarter of total CRC membership.

[28] NACRC, op. cit.

NACRC carried no real authority, there is little doubt that the Association represented the views of many of its members. Community relations officers offered a mixed response when asked if they viewed their organizations as an ethnic-minority pressure group. Only 19 of 39 CROs identified with this role. Conservative CRCs in our sample seemed reluctant, for ideological as well as pragmatic reasons, to identify solely or primarily with non-white interests. Most wished to be seen as racially evenhanded. As one CRO argued:

The CRC must at all costs avoid alienating ordinary . . . [citizens] from its aims and ideals by appearing to always side with the ethnic minorities. If we believe that racism and prejudice are evil then this must equally apply to all sections of the community.

On the other hand, the notion of assuming the role of a non-white pressure group among many progressive CRCs was anathema, implying that CRCs could claim to represent the wide diversity of interests within the non-white community. From the perspective of these committees it would be illegitimate to make this claim in the light of the recent appearance of numerous local non-white voluntary associations, or self-help groups, whose significance for the community relations movement we will discuss below.

CRCS AND NON-WHITE REPRESENTATIVE ASSOCIATIONS

In addition to attracting non-white members and neutralizing the energies of ethnic minorities, CRCs, as we argued above, were expected by the political parties to discourage the political mobilization of ethnic minorities. What of the charge that local committees obstruct the emergence of non-white representative associations, or self-help groups?

Self-help groups, as the name implies, are self-starting organizations which represent the interests or views of segments of the local non-white community. They are, for the most part, small groups which are organized around generational, religious, occupational, or ethnic criteria. Although many of these groups are political in the sense that they make demands of local and national authorities, most are in fact

social welfare organizations. Their principal aim is to represent and/or cater for the interests of their clients directly, thus
circumventing government bodies ostensibly responsible for
performing similar functions.

CRCs officially support non-white self-help groups. Both
the National Association of Community Relations Councils,
the principal spokesman of CRCs, and the Commission for
Racial Equality have urged CRCs to assist the development of
ethnic-minority, grass-roots organizations. Collectively and
individually CRCs have stressed the importance of supporting
non-white community groups:

The . . . [CRC] is very aware of the plight of local community
groups seeking to put their ideas into action through the creation of
projects. . . . The groups require funds and assistance from a variety
of sources and . . . [we are] often able to help as a last resort. Our
small grants are directed each year into those areas where we think
they could be most usefully employed.

[We] try to provide encouragement and support to local youth
groups by helping them with grant applications, problems with
buildings, liaising with the local authority, taking up discrimination
cases, education and employment advice, funding, appearing in
court, and obtaining legal help.

However, in practice, relations between CRCs and self-help
groups have been problematic.

CRCs conflict with ethnic-minority organizations on several fronts. First, local committees compete with self-help
groups for scarce community resources. Although autonomous in the formation of policy, self-help groups often depend
on statutory agencies, including local authorities and the
CRE, for financial aid. CRCs and self-help groups thus seek
funding from the same sources. Second, many self-help group
projects overlap with CRC activities, precipitating tensions
between the two sides over work jurisdiction. This conflict
especially arises in areas where access to local government is
restricted and statutory agencies pursue consultative and
corporatist arrangements in dealing with the non-white
community. In these circumstances, CRCs and self-help
groups vie to be officially recognized as the principal
representative of the non-white community. The third and
most divisive source of conflict is CRC help to these groups.

Aid from Community Relations Councils to local non-white voluntary groups, while helpful in the short term, nevertheless threatens their autonomy. The CRC–self-help group relationship in this respect mirrors the negative side of the CRC–CRE association.

Given these conflicts, whether CRCs inhibit the growth of non-white representative associations is a secondary concern. The central issue is whether self-help groups, in imitating CRCs, desire to be tied to government. For it is only in these circumstances that CRCs and self-help groups are in a competitive relationship, and, in this event, the indefinite growth of both is unlikely. A more pertinent question may be to ask what effect the emergence of non-white community associations will have on the future of CRCs? In order to reach non-white citizens (in a manner CRCs have not), local authorities have increasingly sought to establish a direct relationship with non-white representative associations. The invention of local-government race-relations committees, like those adopted in recent years in the London boroughs of Camden, Islington, and Lewisham, could, if widely imitated by other authorities, decrease the influence of the local committees within the Town Hall. As Prashar and Nicholas report:

With the development of direct consultative initiatives the role of CRCs is beginning to change. Black and other ethnic-minority groups are demanding direct access to local authorities and resent interference by intermediary bodies. The credibility of CRCs is generally very low and none commands the confidence of the black and other ethnic minority groups.[29]

At the very least, the widespread establishment of these committees will make it less necessary for local authorities to liaise with ethnic minorities through CRCs.

The CRE, too, through its direct funding of ethnic-minority self-help groups, is threatening to disassociate itself from CRCs. Apprehension within the community-relations movement over this development has been fuelled by the increasing

---

[29] Prashar and Nicholas, op. cit, pp. 35–6. Where local authorities are convinced that their CRC has a small or insignificant non-white constituency and non-white self-help groups exist, they have been known to discontinue their relationship with local committees.

level of verbal and financial assistance given to these organizations in recent years by the CRE. The Commission has explicitly identified self-help groups as key allies in the fight for racial equality and at least one high-ranking CRE official has indicated that the Commission's support of CRCs will not continue indefinitely.[30] In the fiscal year 1978/9 the CRE allocated £452,095 to 26 ethnic minority organizations; in 1983, £754,663 was distributed to 29 groups. Many of these organizations are located in Greater London where, to the discomfort of the local committees, the largest regional concentration of CRCs can also be found.

CONCLUSIONS

The expansion and evolution of the community-relations movement have been structured, as we have seen, by the strategy of Britain's major political parties to extricate race from local politics. Although Community Relations Councils began as independent, temporary organizations, the parties soon transformed them into quasi-governmental, semi-permanent structures in order to depoliticize race. This objective was not completely achieved; caught between conflicting constituencies, CRCs ultimately failed to satisfy the expectations of the parties. However, in tying CRCs to government and making them politically accountable, the major political parties prevented CRCs from transcending their original role as social-welfare agencies.

Although the inadequacies of CRCs were visible early, it was not until the dissolution of the Conservative and Labour parties' consensus on racial issues during the 1970s that the demise of the community-relations movement could be foreseen.[31] Until 1975 or so CRCs were infrequently criticized; the community-relations movement generally retained the confidence of the major parties. However, with the erosion of the consensus, the adoption by the Conservative party of an illiberal, anti-immigrant posture, and the outbreak of urban riots in 1981 and 1985, the political environment has visibly

[30] Remark made by a CRE officer during author's interview.
[31] See Ch. 6.

altered. Politicians in search of anti-immigrant votes now often portray CRCs as political agents favouring non-whites.[32] Lauded by the parties in the post–1965 period for promoting harmony, many CRCs in the last decade have been accused of exacerbating racial tensions. As many as 10 per cent of CRCs received little or no local-authority financial support in 1985 because of local-authority dissatisfaction with committee actions and/or policy orientation.

The Commission for Racial Equality has recently recognized the shortcomings of CRCs. Accordingly, the CRE has turned to self-help groups who, the Commission hopes, will deliver what CRCs did not. By tightening the reins on CRCs and making it increasingly difficult for these bodies to satisfy the Commission's 'requirements', the CRE appears to be preparing for the day when it will withdraw all financial support from the local committees. In the interim, CRCs are subject to increasing central control, further compromising what remains of the autonomy of the community-relations movement.

The slow eclipse of CRCs, as they give way to other means of representing ethnic minorities, does not necessarily mean that non-whites are better represented in local politics. First, the creation of formal arrangements outside CRCs does not ensure that the interests of non-whites will be regularly incorporated into the political agenda. The recent collapse of dialogue between the local authority and ethnic-minority groups in Liverpool demonstrates that direct consultation does not always precipitate meaningful political change.[33] Moreover, as Prashar and Nicholas caution:

There is a real possibility that these initiatives by local authorities may come to be seen as an updated version of the initiatives of the '60s and '70s when CRCs were created to mediate between statutory bodies and black and other ethnic minority communities. Elaborate, formal structures can sap energy.[34]

[32] Indeed, in a short but pregnant paragraph of his report on the 1981 Brixton disturbances, no less an apolitical figure than Lord Scarman admonished CRCs for forgetting that their 'primary duty is to foster harmony not to undermine it'. *The Brixton Disorders*, Cmnd. 8427, London, HMSO, 1982, p. 110.

[33] See Liverpool Black Caucus, *The Racial Politics of Militant in Liverpool*, London, Runnymede Trust, 1986.

[34] Prasher and Nicholas, op. cit., p. 50.

Just as CRCs were transformed and shaped by their intimate relationship with and financial dependence on local government, so too do many ethnic-minority voluntary associations risk losing their independence to the local authorities. However, as we shall see in the next chapter, in many communities even the partial appropriation of ethnic-minority groups by local government may be preferable to existing arrangements.

4

Ethnic-Minority Representation and Local-Party Competition:

The Case of Ealing Borough

INTRODUCTION

The inability of Community Relations Councils to extricate race from politics completely, even at the height of the Conservative and Labour parties' racial consensus, potentially allowed race-related issues to dominate the political agenda of local communities with substantial ethnic-minority populations. Particularly threatening to the racial consensus was the possibility that non-whites might use their collective voice, in the manner of a conventional interest group, to press their special claims in the local political market-place. In the event, the worst fears of the parties were never realized. Despite the occasional eruption of racial violence in Britain's inner cities, race-related issues have rarely surfaced on local political agendas and non-white interests continue to be under-represented in Town Halls. How the major parties have successfully skirted race issues and neglected the interests of non-whites at the local level with electoral impunity are the central concerns of this chapter.

That race should emerge as a relevant political issue at the local level is not surprising. As Katznelson and Lawrence have pointed out, most race-related subjects are linked with local affairs, especially in the public-policy areas of education, community relations, and housing.[1] As we saw in Chapter 2, the politicization of race locally preceded its emergence as a national concern. Moreover, it is primarily at the sub-national level that the electorate sees the major parties as fulfilling or

[1] Ira Katznelson, *Black Men, White Cities*, London, OUP, 1973, pp. 123–48; and Daniel Lawrence, *Black Migrants, White Natives*, London, CUP, 1974.

falling short of their national promises on race issues. Unlike their colleagues at the national level. local politicians are accountable to a relatively small number of constituents whose daily existence is immediately affected by race-related conflict.

One locality where this conflict has been prolonged and especially acute is the London borough of Ealing (LBE).[2] Several factors make Ealing an interesting case-study of the local politics of race in Britain. The borough, and specifically its Southall area wards, have experienced periodic outbreaks of race-related violence. These incidents have occurred often enough and attracted sufficient local and national media attention to make politicians in Ealing acutely aware of race as a political issue.[3] Second, Ealing has historically had a large ethnic-minority population. According to the 1981 census at least one-quarter of Ealing's population are non-white, including over 40 per cent of all Southall residents (see Table 4.1). Third, since Ealing's amalgamation as a borough in 1964, neither the Conservative nor Labour party has dominated. In 1988 Ealing remains a two-party area, as

TABLE 4.1. *Ealing: population profile 1981*

Parliamentary constituency	Total population	New Commonwealth-born		Population density (pop./hect.)
		Number	% of total population	
Ealing North	92,309	13,200	14.3	42.3
Ealing Acton	84,515	11,832	14.0	50.7
Ealing Southall	103,022	45,020	43.7	60.7
TOTAL	279,846	70,052	25.0	50.4

Source: Office of Population Censuses and Surveys, *Parliamentary Constituency Monitor*, London, OPCS, May 1983.

[2] Ealing is an amalgamation of the formerly autonomous Middlesex boroughs of Acton, Southall and Ealing. The overwhelming majority of non-whites settled in Ealing have ties with the Indian subcontinent.

[3] Since 1964 Ealing has experienced several outbreaks of race-related violence. Undoubtedly the most serious of these incidents were the 1979 and 1981 Southall disturbances which. because of their ferocity and scope, attracted national as well as international press coverage. For an account of the 1979 incidents see the report of the Unofficial Committee of Enquiry, *Southall 23 April 1979*, London, National Council for Civil Liberties, 1980.

Labour has won four and the Conservative party three local elections over the past two decades.

Combined, these factors would appear to elevate race-related issues to a prominent position on the political agenda in Ealing. The closeness of the electoral support of the major parties combined with the inability of the Social and Liberal Democrats to make significant electoral inroads in the borough ostensibly gives the major parties every incentive to address the interests of all of Ealing's sizeable minorities, including non-whites.[4] Yet this has not been the case. Despite apparent political and electoral pressures, local politicians in Ealing have been no more likely than their national counter-parts to address themselves to race-related difficulties. While local politics 'are not simply national politics writ small', in Ealing many of the inadequacies of the major parties at the national level have been mirrored.[5] Paradoxically Ealing's political parties appear to be further removed from the concerns of non-whites than their national counterparts despite the apparently greater stake of the local parties in the conflict surrounding race-related questions.

The central argument of this chapter is that the avoidance of race by the Conservative and Labour parties in Ealing and, concomitantly, their neglect of the borough's non-white population, spring paradoxically from the near-equal representation of the parties in the local Council; as a consequence of their intense electoral struggle, both parties cater disproportionately for the interests of Ealing's electorally marginal areas, often to the detriment of safer wards where most of Ealing's non-white population resides. Although the ethnic-minority community is concentrated in Labour-dominant wards, this does not sufficiently explain its relative lack of political influence nor its difficulty in placing its concerns on the political agenda, since it is not the white working class which makes these areas one-party-dominant but, rather, non-whites who in at least two wards constitute the majority population. Why then cannot non-white electors use their

---

[4] In the May 1986 Council elections the SDP/Liberal Alliance gained only three seats on approximately 17% of the total vote. The electoral support of the Alliance is especially weak in Southall's core wards where most of Ealing's non-white population resides.

[5] Kenneth Newton, *Second City Politics*, London, OUP, 1976, p. 12.

significant numbers to political advantage? Why cannot they offer their votes to the highest party bidder? In circumstances of two-partism where one major party is ideologically or pragmatically constrained from adopting a particular set of interests (as the Conservative party has been with regard to ethnic-minority concerns in Ealing and the nation), excluded groups have only two politically viable alternatives: to support the opposition, however undesirable it may be, or to 'exit' from the conventional political process. In pursuing either course non-whites will enjoy only marginal political influence despite their significant numbers.

Most of the data in this chapter were supplied by Ealing's politicians, including 20 of the borough's elected councillors and its three Members of Parliament. A representative mix of junior and senior politicians from throughout the borough comprised our interview sample of ten Conservative and ten Labour representatives. Each councillor was asked a series of questions on race-related issues. Perhaps the most enlightening aspect of the responses elicited was the responses Ealing's councillors did not offer. As we shall see below, Ealing's politicians generally deny the existence of race-related difficulties and historically have responded to those which cannot be denied by extricating them from party politics. Moreover, whenever non-white interests and those of white voters unavoidably collide, as has frequently occurred over the past decade, electoral considerations dictate that even the most pressing and legitimate claims of the non-white community be subordinated.

RACIAL CONFLICT IN EALING

In its brief history, Ealing has experienced several outbreaks of race-related violence. During the past two decades white and non-white youths, and ethnic minorities, and the police have clashed intermittently, with the most serious incidents resulting in the deaths of non-white youths in 1970 and 1976. In contrast with other London boroughs, however, Ealing's racial violence had rarely if ever been associated with political objectives or protest until the decision of the Conservative

Council to permit a National Front election meeting in the parliamentary constituency of Southall in April 1979. The decision of the Council precipitated a series of violent disturbances in Southall with long-term political repercussions.

With the Council upholding the right of the National Front to assemble, Southall's Indian Workers' Association, Ealing Community Relations Council (ECRC), and other local community groups sponsored a protest march on 22 April, the day before the NF's meeting. Approximately 5,000 people participated in the march, including many of Ealing's most prominent citizens. The anti-Front solidarity of the diverse political, religious, and social groups involved in the march demonstrated the widespread unpopularity of the decision of the Council to let the hall to the NF and subsequently gave impetus to plans for a sit-down strike in the road adjacent to Southall Town Hall on 23 April. The strike, in conjunction with an organized afternoon closing of Asian-owned shops, was intended to demonstrate the anger of Southall residents over the presence of the National Front. However, the sit-down protest never occurred. Instead, violence between the police and hundreds of assembled demonstrators erupted, persisting for most of the afternoon and early evening. Approximately 340 people were eventually arrested and hundreds injured. In the most serious incident of the afternoon a young Anti-Nazi League supporter was fatally beaten by the police.[6]

The disturbances traumatized the residents of Southall, and especially its Indian- and Pakistani-descended population. As one source reported:

There remains a deep unease and insecurity caused by the occurrence of what most people would never have imagined could happen; a sense of hurt, and a disillusion with institutions they wanted to be able to respect. . . .

The politicians have . . . deplored the breach of public order. They have almost as unanimously laid the blame on the supposed arrival in large numbers of outside extremists who launched physical attacks on the police, who incited local residents to do so. They have all praised the police for their restraint and courage. . . . But not one

---

[6] This incident is described in the report of the Unofficial Committee of Inquiry, *The Death of Blair Peach*, London, National Council for Civil Liberties, 1980.

appears to have perceived the necessity for saying something to allay the feelings of alienation produced in the Southall community or even express an understanding of the affront which the day's events had caused.[7]

Indeed, few politicians, local or national, addressed the underlying causes of the violence, with most attributing the events of 23 April to the machinations of anti-authority 'extremists'. The belief in an organized conspiracy was especially prevalent among prominent Conservatives in Ealing.[8]

The reluctance of Ealing's politicians to consider the motivations of the anti-Front protestors induced at least indirectly a replay of the events of 23 April 1979 some two years later. On 3 July 1981, an invasion of Southall's main shopping area by approximately 100 young National Front supporters and their physical and verbal abuse of passers-by precipitated retaliation by a spontaneously mobilized group of Asian youths. Incensed by the protection of the neo-Nazi provocateurs by the police, the non-white youths pelted NF supporters and police with missiles for several hours, causing injury to more than 70 police officers and civilians. In the heat of the battle a local tavern reputed to be a favourite haunt of the neo-Nazis was fire-bombed.

Whatever the cause or causes of the 1979 and 1981 disturbances, one fact is beyond dispute: race is hardly peripheral to local politics in Ealing. In addition to the periodic outbreak of race-related violence and the presence of a sizeable ethnic-minority population in the borough, many public-policy areas, including education, community relations, and housing have historically had a racial dimension, that is, they have directly or indirectly touched upon tensions arising from Ealing's multiracial composition. Despite its obvious salience for Ealing's citizens, however, race has not been historically recognized as a relevant political category by the major political parties in the borough.

DEPOLITICIZING RACE

As a consequence of the higher visibility of race-related issues locally, the Conservative and Labour parties' bipartisan

---

[7] Unofficial Committee of Enquiry, *Southall*, pp. 12–14.   [8] Author's interviews.

consensus at this level was and has been far more nebulous and vulnerable to disintegration than their understanding on race nationally. However, because of the greater prominence of local over national race-related conflict, the local depoliticization strategy of the major parties has outlived in many areas their national racial consensus on race.

(i) Education

Education was among the first public-policy areas to be affected by the settlement of a large ethnic-minority population in Ealing. An early example of the efforts of the parties to extricate race from politics was Labour's adoption of busing in 1963 to disperse the increasing number of non-white students attending Southall's schools. During the 15 years of its implementation, busing enjoyed bipartisan support as the Conservatives continued the policy during their 1968–71 tenure in office. Busing was intended to prevent schools in Southall from becoming predominantly non-white, an inevitable outcome given the comparatively high fertility rate of the areas's youthful, ethnic-minority population. Although only 15 per cent of Southall children were officially classified as 'immigrant' in 1964, at least one school in the area had a non-white student population of over 50 per cent, and white parents were soon putting increasing pressure on the Town Hall to reduce the proportion of non-white pupils in Southall's classrooms. Unlike similar arrangements adopted in the United States during the 1960s and 1970s the primary goal of Ealing's dispersal plans was not to provide equal educational opportunity for Southall's non-white schoolchildren. Consequently, local officials failed to monitor the educational performance of either non-white or white students after busing was implemented.[9]

While dispersal partially allayed white anxieties, it skirted the two most serious problems confronting the educational system of the area. It failed, first of all, to address the long-term problem of racial integration within Southall's schools,

[9] See Campaign Against Racism and Fascism/Southall Rights, *Southall: The Birth of a Black Community*, London, Institute of Race Relations and Southall Rights, 1981, p. 32.

postponing only temporarily the inevitable conflict arising from the high birth rate of the non-white community, and hence, the rising proportion of non-whites in local classrooms. Secondly, dispersal did not satisfy the escalating demand for school places, as the school-aged population in Southall predictably outstripped the supply of available classroom places in the 1960s and 1970s. Rather:

Local education became second-class education as the Council . . . claimed no money at all from the central government for the provision of new primary school places. In 1975, when it was estimated that there were 3,000 more primary school children than places in Southall, and at least six new schools were needed, only one was being built.[10]

Under pressure from the non-white community, the Labour Council did initiate the construction of two new secondary schools in Southall in 1978. By this time, however, the political utility of dispersal had already been played out; Southall's rapidly changing demographics (by 1976 over two-thirds of all children under 14 in Southall's Glebe and Northcote wards were non-white), wider acceptance of non-whites by the area's shrinking white majority, and the politicization of busing itself had made dispersal politically imprudent.

(ii) Community relations

As noted in the previous chapter, a key element in the national strategy of the Conservative and Labour parties to depoliticize race was their manipulation of Community Relations Councils. In order to extricate race from local politics, the parties supported CRCs as apolitical outlets for non-white participation in community affairs, with these organizations acting as buffers between non-whites and the predominantly white, local political establishment. In Ealing, the major parties followed the national pattern, financially supporting the local CRC to deflect race-related issues away from local government. This strategy was more difficult to pursue in Ealing than in other communities, however, because of

[10] Campaign Against Racism and Facism/Southall Rights, *Southall: The Birth of a Black Community*, p. 32.

political orientation of the Ealing Community Relations Council. Since its founding before 1963, Ealing Community Relations Council (formerly Southall International Friendship Committee and Ealing International Friendship Committee) has enjoyed an affinity with Labour. Labour councillors were among the first individuals represented on ECRC's management committee and, with the assistance of Labour, Southall International Friendship Committee was transformed into a borough-wide organization. The Conservative party, in contrast, historically has attached stringent conditions to its support of the Committee. Annoyed by ECRC's outspoken criticism of Enoch Powell, the 1968 Immigrants Act, and local busing, the local Conservative leadership assumed office in 1968 intimating that it might withdraw ECRC's local-authority grant as a penalty for its persistent intervention in politics.[11] The Conservatives argued that the ECRC had undermined community relations by publicly challenging local and national government policies. According to Conservative leaders, the ECRC's appropriate role was that of an advice bureau or welfare organization rather than a public advocate for ethnic-minority interests.

Labour's successive victories in the 1971 and 1974 local elections temporarily defused this conflict until 1978 when the Conservative party again assumed control of the Council. Under a new leader the Conservatives established the terms for the continuance of financial support of the Committee: either the ECRC should extricate itself from politics or it would forfeit its local-authority grant. After a series of public exchanges between the two sides during the winter of 1980–1, the Conservative leadership put its decision to withdraw the ECRC's local-authority grant to a vote in the Council chamber. Over the strenuous objections of the Labour party, the Conservative Council withdrew the ECRC's local-authority funding in the spring of 1981.

Why did the Conservative party withdraw its aid after more than a decade of conditional support? Why the disparity in the major parties' posture on the ECRC? To understand the

[11] See M. J. Hill and R. M. Issacharoff, *Community Action and Race Relations*, London, OUP, 1971, pp. 222–3.

divergence in the Conservative and Labour parties' approach to community relations, it is necessary to examine the bases of the parties' electoral support between 1965 and 1982.

RACE AND THE CHANGING ELECTORAL MAP IN EALING

As noted above, neither the Conservative nor the Labour party has dominated Ealing's politics; both parties have always been within striking distance of controlling the borough Council, as Labour has won four of seven local elections. Yet, while the two main parties have enjoyed electoral parity across the borough, they have not competed on equal terms within the borough's wards. Rather, between 1965 and 1977, Ealing neatly divided into three distinct electoral areas: (a) nine Labour wards, including Southall proper, on the western edge of the borough; (b) eight Conservative-dominated wards in central Ealing; (c) the Labour-controlled East, Heathfield, and Southfield wards on Ealing's eastern border. In the first four borough elections between 1965 and 1977 Labour overwhelmingly dominated east and west Ealing, winning 110 of 144 seats in the dozen wards during this period (see Map 1). Over the same period

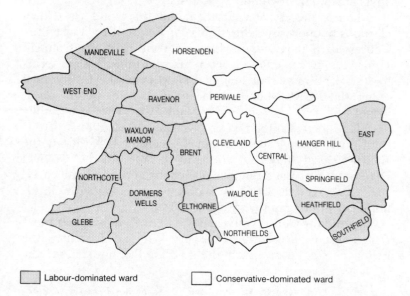

☐ Labour-dominated ward   ☐ Conservative-dominated ward

MAP 1. Ealing: major-party support by ward, 1965–1977

Conservative candidates captured 95 per cent of all the seats in central-Ealing wards.

Moreover, the electoral dominance of east and west Ealing by Labour was even greater than it first appears. If the large, and highly exceptional,[12] Conservative victory of 1968 is excluded, the extent of Labour's hold over the two areas is fully revealed. In its combined Council victories of 1965, 1971, and 1974, Labour captured 105 of 108 total seats in east and west Ealing, while losing only a single Southall ward in 1965. Moreover, even when losing office Labour continued its hold over west Ealing; of 66 possible seats between 1971 and 1982 in the eight wards of Mandeville, West End, Waxlow Manor, Northcote, Glebe, Dormers Wells, Brent, and Elthorne, Labour captured 65. Only the successful campaign of an independent candidate in the Southall ward of Northcote in 1978 prevented Labour from making a clean sweep of west Ealing in the last five elections.

East and west Ealing contain most of the borough's working-class and non-white residents (see Table 4.2). In

TABLE 4.2. *Ealing: population profile by geographical area, 1976*

	West	Central	East
Wards:seats	9:27	8:24	3:9
Per cent of total Ealing non-white population	69	22	9
Per cent of total Ealing population	46	41	13
Per cent non-white	27	10	12
Per cent households renting Council accommodation	29	9	60
Per cent unskilled manual labourers (of total working population)	23	10	17

Source: London Borough of Ealing, *Ealing Sample Census of Population 1976*, London, LBE, 1977.

west Ealing's nine wards, for example, over 22 per cent of the working population was classified as unskilled in 1976,[13]

[12] Labour's débâcle in Ealing in 1968 was, indeed, part of a larger anti-Labour swing nationally. Of the 3,222 seats available in the 1968 local elections Labour captured 450, on a post-war low of 29.8% of the vote. Labour's disastrous performance was primarily attributable to the unpopularity of the Wilson government.

[13] As reported in London Borough of Ealing, *Ealing Sample Census of Population 1976*, London, LBE, 1977.

compared to 10.4 per cent in Conservative-controlled central Ealing. Similarly, while 10 per cent of central-Ealing residents were counted as non-white, more than one-quarter of west Ealing's population originated from the New Commonwealth. Almost 70 per cent of the borough's total non-white population in 1976 were housed in west Ealing, and this area had more than three times as many non-white residents as central Ealing. As much as 75 per cent of Ealing's non-white population historically have resided in Labour-controlled wards.

In the 1960s the Conservative party had not yet conceded the electoral dominance of Southall by Labour. Primarily for this reason, the Conservatives were reluctant to withdraw the ECRC's local-authority grant.[14] Contrary to Conservative hopes, however, Labour's hold over west Ealing, and especially Southall, grew stronger. The rising percentage of ethnic-minority voters in Southall's core wards (Waxlow Manor, Dormers Wells, Glebe, and Northcote) and the propensity of these voters to support Labour in overwhelming numbers,[15] dimmed Conservative-party prospects of making electoral inroads in west Ealing. Indeed, only after the persistent failure of the Conservatives to undercut Labour's electoral support in Southall and the collapse of a Conservative Anglo-Asian Society in the mid–1970s[16] did the party lose interest in utilizing the ECRC as a bridge to the non-white community. Given the ECRC's criticisms of local authority policies, the Conservative party finally acted upon its long-standing threat to withdraw the ECRC's funding.

With the abandonment of the non-white vote in west Ealing by local Conservatives and the increasing hostility evinced by the Conservative party nationally toward non-white immigrants,[17] Ealing's ethnic-minority voters were left with no acceptable electoral alternative to Labour. Virtually by default, Labour has maintained its electoral hold over the

[14] See Hill and Issacharoff, op. cit., p. 221.

[15] Exact figures are not available, but there is little reason to doubt the contention of local politicians that non-whites support Labour in percentages of between 80 and 90.

[16] This Association was one of a number nationally which were supported by Conservative party Central Office in the early 1970s.

[17] See A. M. Messina, 'Race and Party Competition in Britain: Policy Formation in the Post-Consensus Period', *Parliamentary Affairs*, 38.4, Autumn 1985, 423–36.

non-white community in the 1980s. Yet the party cannot simply take the non-white vote for granted; to retain all of its Southall seats safely, Labour needs to ensure non-white voters remain willing to turn out to vote. Primarily for this reason, Labour continues to support verbally the ECRC in its conflict with the Conservatives. Supporting the ECRC is a safe strategy by which Labour can appear to advocate ethnic-minority interests without antagonizing white voters.

During the 1980s Labour has trodden a fine line between consolidating its base of non-white support in Southall and reaching out elsewhere for the seats necessary to attain an overall Council majority. Since Southall's core wards represent only 21 per cent of all Council seats Labour cannot simply rely on this area for electoral support. The requirement to broaden the party's base of support was all the more pressing after 1978 when Labour lost most of its east Ealing strongholds (see Map 2), and, with them, control of Ealing Council. Since 1978, Labour has had to work hard to retain all of its Southall support and to recapture several seats in east Acton in order to remain electorally competitive.

The somewhat unexpected success of the Conservatives in

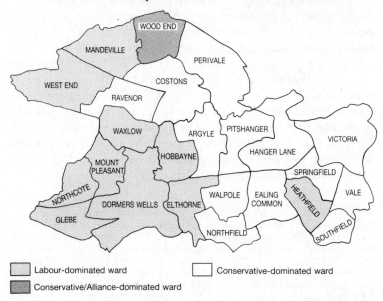

MAP 2. Ealing: major-party support by ward, 1978–1985

east Ealing in 1978 and 1982 created a new pattern of electoral competition. As against the previous pattern, in which Labour, dominating east and west Ealing, was the borough's 'natural' majority party while the Conservatives' dominance was restricted to central Ealing, the new electoral map indicates that the Conservatives were transformed into the majority party by winning the wards of Ravenor in the west and Southfield, Vale, and Victoria in east Acton. All four wards had previously been in Labour's camp for most of the period between 1965 and 1977 and, with a combined seat total of ten, offered Labour its best opportunity to regain the Council majority. Indeed, Labour succeeded in regaining control of the Council in May 1986 by winning the wards of Vale and Victoria. The success of Labour in these wards and its sweep of Springfield's three seats in 1986 cemented the party's victory and further intensified the Conservative and Labour parties' electoral competition for east Ealing.

NON-WHITE INTERESTS AND THE PUBLIC-POLICY AGENDA

East Acton's status as a marginal electoral region in the 1970s not surprisingly enhanced the political importance of the area. Since it potentially can decide the parliamentary balance, both major parties have been sensitive to issues which might affect their political standing in Acton. Such sensitivity has been manifested in the adoption by the parties of policies to court Acton's constituents as well as their avoidance of issues which might alienate this bloc of voters. Neither political party has had strong incentives to address issues significant for Ealing's ethnic minorities, since such concerns are unlikely to appeal to Acton's predominantly white electorate and occasionally conflict with the interests of these voters.[18]

---

[18] The ability of Acton's non-whites to gain political leverage in this electorally marginal area is inhibited by two factors. The first is that there are too few non-white voters. From the mid–1970s no single Acton ward had a non-white population of more than 7.5% and four of seven wards had no more than 4%. A second, less important, obstacle is the fact that non-white voters overwhelmingly support Labour. At least one study has estimated that only 19% of Acton's Asian voters, a more Conservative-inclined group than West Indians, supported the Conservative party in the 1979 general election. M. Anwar, *Votes and Policies*, London, CRE, 1980, p. 46.

(i) Multiracial or religious education?

One important issue to Acton residents in the early 1980s was the fate of Twyford High School. Although the Council abandoned busing in 1978, several state schools in the borough continued to attract a multiracial student body. The most successful of these schools was Twyford High School, which catered for the educational needs of Acton's ethnically diverse school population until its controversial sale to the Church of England in 1981. The reasons given by the Conservative Council for its decision to sell Twyford were the growing number of vacant places at the school as a consequence of Acton's declining school-aged population and the Council's preference for the establishment of a Church of England middle school in the borough. The Conservative Council emphasized that the area lacked an established Anglican high school to educate the 100 school children in the borough already attending Anglican secondary schools outside Ealing. The addition of a denominational high school offered the opportunity for a complete Church education within the borough.

This educational opportunity was, however, relevant only to the white Anglican community in Acton since few of Twyford's non-white pupils were interested in a Church of England education.[19] Yet despite opposition to the sale among Twyford's staff and many ethnic-minority parents, the Conservative Council was not inclined to consider Twyford's value as a multiracial educational institution because of the popularity of the sale among Acton's vocal Anglican community. Not coincidentally, Conservative councillors in Acton were among the strongest advocates of the transfer of Twyford to the Church of England.[20]

The Labour leadership vehemently opposed the sale of Twyford, but for reasons that were not always consistent. Labour councillors principally objected to selling the school on four grounds. First, religious education should not be encouraged:

The Church of England made no original application to be involved

---

[19] Few non-whites are Anglicans.
[20] Author's interviews.

in the Ealing school system years ago. It's not appropriate for religious denominations to use borough schools.

Equal opportunity should be provided to all children. I'm totally against selective, private education. It would divide the community along religious lines.

I am opposed to any extension of denominational education because in the end it would mean having separate schools for every religion. I do not believe that a society which segregates its children by religion in their formative years will help those children live in harmony and understanding as adults.

Second, Twyford was a successful, multiracial educational institution which could not be replaced:

Is it any wonder that the issue of denominational education has become one of public concern when . . . [the Tories] have sold off a successful multiracial high school to the Church of England against the wishes of parents, staff, pupils and among community organizations?

Third, declining school rolls could permit, given the retention of Twyford, a reduction in the student–teacher ratio in the Borough:

If rolls are falling then classes should be reduced to a maximum of 25 pupils.

Falling rolls are a golden chance to improve the educational experience and to give proper attention to every child. A maximum of 25 children per class is best.

We could have developed our schools on smaller classes, providing a better education.

And fourth, public assets should not be sold:

The Labour party line is to resist the sale of any schools in this borough. Schools could instead be used for youth clubs and nursery provision.

The least popular of these positions among Labour councillors was the value of Twyford to Ealing borough as a multiracial institution. Only one Labour councillor out of ten mentioned the importance of this factor when questioned about the controversial sale. In contrast, 40 per cent cited the value of retaining Twyford to alleviate classroom overcrowding. The reluctance of Labour politicians to highlight Twyford's value as a multiracial institution, despite the school's national reputation, undoubtedly stemmed from the desire of the party to avoid antagonizing white Acton voters favourable to the sale. By framing its opposition to the transfer of Twyford to the Anglican Church within the framework of the party's traditional commitment to comprehensive education and public property ownership, Labour attempted to address the concerns of Twyford's non-white supporters in a manner acceptable to whites.

(ii) Housing

A second major issue dividing Ealing's non-white and white community, and one pitting Ealing's less prosperous, predominantly non-white areas against more gentrified parts of the borough, is housing. Despite its deserved reputation as a comparatively wealthy, outer London borough, Ealing has found itself annually since 1976 among municipalities with an acute housing deficit, the depth of which is reflected in the length of the borough's council-house waiting-list, the queue of eligible households seeking to rent publicly owned accommodation. In each of the five years before 1981 Ealing ranked among the top three outer London boroughs with the greatest number of citizens on its housing list, as its housing deficit was virtually double that of other outer London boroughs in 1976, 1980, and 1983.[21] According to one independent report Ealing had '4,400 fewer homes than people to fill them' in 1980.[22] This figure excludes an estimated 8,400 dwellings judged by the former Greater London Council Authority as unfit for healthy human habitation.[23]

The housing shortage in Ealing has undoubtedly caused the greatest hardship to the residents of Southall, where an overwhelming majority of Ealing's non-white citizens are residentially concentrated in the five wards of Dormers Wells,

---

[21] See the annual surveys of housing waiting-lists provided by the housing pressure-group Shelter.

[22] Ealing Housing Aid Service, *Southall Ignored*, London, EHAS, 1980.

[23] As cited in the document *Housing Investment Programme Strategy Statement 1986/87*, London, London Borough of Ealing 1985.

Glebe, Mount Pleasant, Northcote, and Waxlow. According
to the 1981 national census, more than 23 per cent of the
borough's total population resides in these wards, including
55 per cent of Ealing's ethnic-minority population. By Ealing
Council's own estimates, 9.1 per cent of all households in
Northcote and Glebe wards have more than 1.5 persons per
room,[24] with 40 per cent of the properties in Northcote
occupied by more than one household. Thirteen per cent of all
Glebe and Northcote families do not have such basic
amenities as the exclusive use of an inside toilet, compared to
a borough-wide average of 7.5 per cent. In the worst sector of
Northcote's core area, 24 per cent of all families lack any fixed
bath or shower. Among these households, some 8 per cent had
no access to hot water and 7 per cent no indoor toilet as
recently as 1978.

Despite the severity of Ealing's, and specifically Southall's,
housing shortage and the poor condition of many existing
dwellings, Ealing Council since the mid–1970s has decreased
substantially the level of public investment in new house
building (see Table 4.3). In 1984, for example, the Conservative Council estimated less than 100 council houses would be
constructed in the fiscal year 1984–5, 900 fewer than were
completed by a financially austere Labour administration in
1977–8. Moreover, in 1978–9, the Conservative Council
deliberately neglected to spend 30 per cent of the housing
monies made available to it by the central government, a
move intended to reduce local-authority expenditure and
responsibility for house construction and maintenance. In
1979–80, the Council once again failed to utilize its full
housing allocation, underspending its central government
grant by 15 per cent. Ealing's frugality was in sharp contrast
with other London boroughs, which on average underspent
their housing allocation by only 12 per cent in 1978–9 and 1.2
per cent in 1979–80.[25] This policy may have circumvented
Ealing's statutory obligation under section 76 of the 1957
National Housing Act which states: 'It shall be the duty of the
authority . . . to prepare and submit a report showing . . . the
number of new houses required in order to abate over-

---

[24] *Housing Investment Programme Strategy Statement* 1986/87.
[25] As reported on, the *Skin Programme*, London Weekend Television, 16 Nov. 1980.

TABLE 4.3. *Ealing: housing construction and expenditure, 1973–1985*

Year	Governing party	Units built	Expenditure 1975 £ million*
1973–4	Labour	205	n/a
1974–5	Labour	159	13.6
1975–6	Labour	n/a	15.5
1976–7	Labour	1108	13.9
1977–8	Labour	1007	6.9
1978–9	Conservative	522	5.9
1979–80	Conservative	376	7.3
1980–1	Conservative	572	7.0
1981–2	Conservative	299	5.4
1982–3	Conservative	105	4.6
1983–4	Conservative	117	n/a
1984–5	Conservative	89	n/a

* Capital expenditure on the acquisition, construction, improvement, and conversion of council-owned sites and dwellings.

Sources: Ealing Housing Aid Service, *You've Got No Chance*, London, EHAS, 1980; LBE, *Housing Investment Programmes*, 1976–85; LBE, *Housing Committee Abstract of the Accounts*, 1975–83.

crowding . . . and unless they are satisfied that the number of houses will be otherwise provided, to prepare and submit . . . proposals for the provision' of new dwellings.[26]

While in opposition, Ealing's Labour group vigorously resisted the housing cuts of the Conservatives. Ninety per cent of the Labour councillors interviewed, for example, mentioned Ealing's housing crisis as one of the most urgent problems facing the borough. The poor quality of the housing stock in Ealing and LBE's housing shortage were, in fact, cited more often by Labour councillors than any other major issue. Yet, despite its apparent sensitivity to this issue, Labour in office too was quite cautious in tackling Ealing's housing crisis, as Table 4.3 illustrates. At the end of Labour's administrative tenure in 1978, Council capital spending on housing declined, in both real and relative terms, from the level spent four years previously, despite a 9 per cent increase in the borough's rather lengthy council-house waiting-list. During 1977–8, only

[26] As cited in Ealing Housing Aid Service, *A Disaster Course for the 80's*, London, EHAS, 1979, pp. 24–5.

140 housing units were started, almost 800 fewer than were begun in 1975–6.

Labour's modest building programme, like that of the Conservatives, cannot be attributed to a lack of financial resources. In the three fiscal years preceding 1979, Ealing, like other outer London boroughs, received generous central-government housing grants,[27] moneys which would have facilitated a capital-expansion programme. Raising rates to alleviate housing stress in Southall was not, however, given a high priority. Labour's former housing spokesman justified the decision to hold down rates in terms of the party's consideration for race relations:

[We] consider[ed] the impact of the rate increases on . . . matters like race relations and how the citizenry as a whole . . . [would] have reacted to a large rate increase confined merely to dealing with a severe problem in housing. These are matters which one would have had to consider very carefully and I think on balance we would not necessarily have served the best interests of the community in Southall by adopting an extreme view.[28]

While Labour's spokesman explicitly cited its potential impact on 'race relations', the decision of the Council to hold down rates was undoubtedly influenced by electoral consider-ations. The white backlash which, Labour feared, rate increases might precipitate would have occurred in the more prosperous areas including the electorally critical Acton wards. Given this prospect, Labour chose to restrict overall Council expenditure and reduce rates rather than to be seen to be committing 'excessive' funds to alleviate Southall's housing stress. Despite the housing crisis in Southall, the Council under both Labour and Conservative administrations success-fully kept borough rates among the lowest in the country from the mid-1970s onwards.

The explicit disregard of Southall's housing crisis by the Con-servative party was particularly evident in its housing strategy during the 1980s. Of the less than 100 council houses con-structed by the Conservative Council in 1984–5, most were built as sheltered units for the elderly and handicapped. Acton, not Southall, received the lion's share of the new units. The Conservative Council's justification for concentrating shel-

---

[27] The *Skin Programme*, 16 Nov.   [28] Ibid.

tered housing construction in Acton rested on the findings of
its 1980 population survey which projected a significant *future*
demand for housing for the elderly as the median population
age in Acton steadily rose to 1991.[29] This reasoning effectively
ignored the reality that the majority of the waiting-list
applicants in Ealing during the 1980s have been single people
and childless couples seeking one-bedroom flats. Indeed, the
Council also ignored evidence from its own survey which
projected a net decline in Acton households between 1976 and
1986 and a net increase in Southall households of between 4
and 69 per cent in individual wards. Given the flawed logic of
the official explanation of the party, the principal motivation
of the Conservatives for concentrating housing construction in
Acton was probably to court white, elderly voters.

The second prong of the Conservatives' local and national
housing policy during the 1980s—selling council-owned
accommodation to sitting tenants at below market value—
exacerbated Ealing's housing difficulties.[30] Between 1979 and
1981 the Conservative Council sold more than 1,100 housing
units from its stock of 22,000 dwellings, thus reducing Ealing's
supply of affordable rental property. The Conservative party
hoped to gain politically on two scores by selling council
property. First, the party hoped to convert Labour-inclined
council tenants into Tory-voting home owners. Defections
from Labour would have been especially welcome among east
Acton council tenants, who comprised up to 33 per cent of all
households in the marginal wards of Vale and Victoria. And
secondly, the reduction in council-owned accommodation
decreased local-authority housing maintenance costs and
subsidies, thus allowing lower rates for private home-owners
and businesses. Since approximately 60 per cent of all
households in Conservative-controlled wards are owner-
occupied, the Conservative party could only profit politically
by reducing or stabilizing rates.

Ealing's Labour party, in line with the positions of Labour
nationally, consistently opposed the sale of council houses.
However, like its resistance to the transfer of Twyford High

[29] London Borough of Ealing, *Ealing in the Future*, London, LBE, 1980.
[30] Ealing's Conservative group enthusiastically complied with the policy adopted
by the 1979–83 Thatcher government to sell council houses to sitting tenants at rates
which vary according to the tenant's length of residence.

School to the Anglican Church, Labour leaders cautiously framed their opposition within a context acceptable to Ealing's white population, that is, the party avoided addressing the discriminatory implications of the Conservatives' housing strategy. Labour's housing posture was further complicated by the popularity of council house sales among many of the party's traditional working-class supporters. The party especially stood to lose votes on this issue in east Acton where, as cited above, approximately a third of all households in the Vale and Victoria wards were eligible to purchase council-owned accommodation at affordable prices.

CONCLUSIONS

In the London borough of Ealing, the Conservative and Labour parties have persistently failed to address, and indeed have actively avoided, race-related issues. Generally, the financial support of Ealing Community Relations Council by the parties was intended to extricate race from politics, while, in the area of education, non-white children were dispersed to allay the fears of white parents. That the major parties managed to avoid race-related controversy in a community where the issue is salient is contrary to expectations, especially given Ealing's status as a two-party borough. Indeed, despite a sizeable non-white population in Ealing, the incidence of sporadic race-related violence, and public-policy areas where the subject is obviously relevant, race has historically played little role in the struggle of the Conservative and Labour parties for elected office.

How the major parties avoid racial issues and, more specifically, neglected the interests of non-white voters, are primarily explained by the segmented nature of their electoral support. While the parties have been and are competitive at the macro-electoral level, they have not competed in all of Ealing's constituent areas. For all practical purposes they have not competed politically at all in Southall. The consequences of the political and electoral domination of the area by Labour are fairly obvious. While Conservatives wrote off Southall and neglected the interests of its residents when in office, Labour often took the area for granted. Labour addressed the concerns of its Southall constituents only when they did not conflict with the interests of marginal Acton voters or when they coincided with Labour's traditional ideological commitments. The grounds on which Labour resisted the sale of public assets, such as council houses, pointedly illustrates this latter tendency.

How representative is the case of Ealing? Is the political pattern of avoiding and depoliticizing race-related issues evident in other communities with sizeable ethnic-minority populations? Previous case studies of Labour- and Conservative-controlled communities and areas where no party is dominant reveal that Ealing is not unique.[31] In a fairly comprehensive study of local politics in Birmingham in the early 1970s, for example, Newton discovered:

For the two main parties, race and colour have not been much of an electoral issue, even during the ten years during which Birmingham has acquired a notorious reputation as a centre for anti-immigrant feelings. . . . Not only have most candidates for the two main parties been unwilling to campaign on the race issue, but . . . Council members have not taken much trouble to attract the immigrant vote or even to find out very much about it. . . . Most Council members seem to feel that they can get by quite adequately without making any special appeal to immigrant groups.[32]

A recent analysis of non-white political disadvantage in Liverpool, under both Liberal- and Labour-led Councils, reached broadly similar conclusions, despite the presence of a large and politically active ethnic-minority population and the occurrence of serious race-related violence in that community in 1981 and 1985.[33] In some localities, especially within Greater London, non-whites have recently achieved greater access to local decision-makers than in the past. However, on the whole, Young's observation that 'ethnic pluralism, with all its ambiguities and conflicts of value, has yet to be reflected

[31] See e.g. K. Young and Naomi Connelly, *Policy and Practice in the Multi-Racial City*, London, Policy Studies Institute, 1981; and B. D. Jacobs, *Black Politics and Urban Crisis in Britain*, Cambridge, CUP, 1986.

[32] Newton, op. cit., p. 214.

[33] Liverpool Black Caucus, *The Racial Politics of Militant in Liverpool*, London, Runnymede Trust, 1986. See also Steve Platt, 'The Liberals in Power', *New Society*, 11 Sept. 1987, 8–9.

in the political agenda' is the rule at the local level in Britain even when, as we have seen in Ealing, electoral circumstances would appear to favour the exercise of meaningful non-white political influence.[34]

What generalizations can be drawn from the case of Ealing? The most obvious is that electorally competitive two-partism does not automatically ensure that the interests of even sizeable minorities will be represented politically; even under seemingly favourable circumstances, the concerns of minorities in a two-party system might be 'aggregated' but not necessarily 'articulated'.[35] Moreover, contrary to Downs's expectations,[36] in a first-past-the-post electoral system where two major parties enjoy rough parity, as has been recently true in Ealing and Britain as a whole in the post-war period, parties will not attempt to maximize votes but seats, for governments are made and govern on the basis of the size of their legislative representation.[37] The logic of this situation virtually dictates that issues—in Ealing or the country— which threaten to undermine party strategies to maximize seats will often be suppressed, irrespective of how many individual votes might be 'lost' or voters disillusioned. The persistent avoidance of salient issues by parties is, of course, not without cost, as race-related violence in Ealing and the other parts of the country in the 1980s have demonstrated. However, in the short term such costs will not normally include disturbing the balance of party strength in the legislature.

[34] K. Young, 'Ethnic Pluralism and the Policy Agenda in Britain', in, N. Glazer and K. Young (eds.), *Ethnic Pluralism and Public Policy*, London, Heinemann, 1983, p. 288.

[35] See Ivor Crewe, 'Representation and Ethnic Minorities in Britain', in, Glazer and Young (eds.), op. cit., pp. 258–84.

[36] The notion of political parties as 'vote maximizers' was, of course, central to A. Downs's understanding of inter-party competition, *An Economic Theory of Democracy*, New York, Harper and Row, 1957.

[37] G. Sartori, *Parties and Party Systems: A Framework for Analysis*, vol. i, Cambridge, CUP, 1976, p. 186.

5

Race and the Emergence of Anti-Consensus Forces:

Enoch Powell, the National Front, and the Anti-Nazi League

INTRODUCTION

When party competition in a two-party system diminishes, when inter-party policy consensus prevails which preserves the status quo and suppresses public, political discussion, then intra-party schisms, political disaffection by the electorate, and extra-parliamentary political protest almost inevitably result. As Schoen has persuasively argued:

All major segments of the electorate must feel that their interests are being adequately represented. Voters must also feel that the choices presented by the political parties are meaningful. If neither of these functions is performed, the result is likely to be protest, apathy, or support for third parties and extreme movements.[1]

There is little question that large numbers of Britons in the 1960 and 1970s felt that their political interests were not adequately represented, and that the major parties did not offer meaningful policy alternatives. Apart from the 50 per cent who saw the major parties as 'all much of a muchness' (see Table 1.1), over two-thirds of the electorate believed that the voters did not exercise sufficient influence over the course of public policy and approximately 33 per cent concluded that 'neither the Conservative nor Labour party represents the views of people like me'.[2] Indeed, the British electorate's

---

[1] Douglas E. Schoen, *Enoch Powell and the Powellites*, New York, St. Martin's, 1977, p. 233.
[2] Ibid., p. 249.

increasing distrust of government and detachment from the major parties were two of the most prominent political trends of the 1960s and 1970s. [3] As public confidence in the parties eroded, disaffected citizens turned to individual and organizational critics of the parties' political consensus. Hence, in the 1960s and 1970s Britain witnessed a modest explosion of Powellites, Bennites, and a plethora of extra-parliamentary ginger groups and protest movements.[4]

In this chapter we examine the political consequences of the neglect by the Conservative and Labour parties of race-related issues. We focus on the three most visible and politically influential opponents of the Conservative and Labour parties' consensus on race: Enoch Powell MP, the National Front, and the Anti-Nazi League. Our argument is that the efforts of the parties to depoliticize race precipitated the emergence and fed the popularity of these representatives of anti-consensus sentiment. By addressing popular concerns and highlighting the shortcomings of the major parties on race, these opponents of the consensus implicitly laid the groundwork for the renewal of party competition in this area of public policy.[5]

RACE AND THE RISE OF ENOCH POWELL

There was no more vocal, politically influential, or visible critic in the 1960s and 1970s of the post-war political consensus than the Conservative MP, Enoch Powell. His opposition to collectivist politics, devolution for Northern Ireland, Keynesian economics, and British entry into the European Economic Community pitted Powell against virtually every major politician associated with the post-war political consensus and was primarily responsible for elevating his public standing to a level reached by few of his peers.[6]

[3] See e.g. Bö Sarlvik and Ivor Crewe, *Decade of Dealignment*, London, CUP, 1983.
[4] See e.g. Richard Taylor and Colin Pritchard, *The Protest Makers*, Oxford, Pergamon, 1980; and A. M. Messina, 'Toward an Alternative Explanation for British Party Decay', unpublished paper, 1986.
[5] Christopher T. Husbands, *Racial Exclusionism and the City*, London, Allen and Unwin, 1983, p. 20.
[6] Schoen, op. cit., p. 276.

At its peak, Powell's support in the electorate cut across political party, region, and class, reflecting 'a more truly national constituency than that possessed by any of the parties, the Liberals not excepted'.[7] At one time or another, at least three-quarters of the electorate endorsed his maverick political views and 20 per cent hoped that he would become prime minister. Moreover, Powell's political influence could be converted into votes:

The Butler–Stokes [panel] data from 1970 and 1974 clearly demonstrated that Powell played a decisive role in winning the 1970 election for the Tories and came back to make an important contribution to the Labour victory in February 1974. . . . Influence of this sort is probably unprecedented in British political history.[8]

Almost single-handedly Powell prepared the intellectual groundwork for the emergence of Margaret Thatcher as Conservative party leader in 1975. Much of the current Thatcher 'revolution' was prefigured in the public-policy positions advocated by Powell in the late 1960s.[9]

Of all the major issues associated with Powell and 'Powellism' it was race which struck the most responsive chord in the electorate. As a direct result of his 'rivers of blood' speech and dismissal from the shadow cabinet (see Chapter 2), Powell became closely identified in the public mind with illiberal racial sentiment between 1968 and 1970.[10] As Table 5.1 indicates, supporters of Powell were somewhat more politically alienated than the electorate as a whole. But general political alienation structured popular attitudes toward Powell less than race-related issues.[11] Although alienation increased in importance as an explanation for Powellism after 1970, it never superseded race. Powell initially gained stature as a national politician because of his virulent opposition to non-white immigration and the parties' racial consensus.[12] He subsequently used his notoriety and credibility on race to attack the EEC, the trade unions, party élites,

[7] Ibid., p. 195.
[8] Ibid., p. 276.
[9] Ibid., pp. 146–7. See also T. E. Utley, 'Thatcher's Debt to Powell,' *The Times*, 15 June 1987, 10.
[10] Schoen, op. cit., pp. 241–2.
[11] Ibid., pp. 252–5.
[12] See Paul Foot, *The Rise of Enoch Powell*, Harmondsworth, Penguin, 1969, p. 116.

TABLE 5.1. *General and 'Powellite' opinion on government, MPs, and immigration, 1969–1970 (% of respondents)*

	1969			1970		
	All	Powell-ites	Non-Powellites	All	Powell-ites	Non-Powellites
(1) Government does not pay much attention to the people*	62	69	59			
(2) MPs do not pay much attention to the people*	36	47	33			
(3) Too many immigrants let in	85	99	81	84	97	80
(4) Feel very strongly about the number of immigrants	54	78	47	49	74	40
(5) Immigrants a neighbourhood problem	13	28	9	11	16	9
(6) Opposed to anti-discrimination legislation*	30	38	27			

* This opinion was not sought in 1970.

Source: Butler–Stokes panel study data as published in Douglas Schoen, *Enoch Powell and the Powellites*, New York, St. Martin's, 1977, tables 11.2 and 11.3.

and other frequent targets of criticism within the British electorate.

Several scholars have argued that Powell's strident campaign against non-white immigration between 1968 and 1974 effectively dissolved the Conservative and Labour parties' racial consensus.[13] By overtly appealing to anti-immigrant public sentiment and by associating the Conservative party with racial illiberalism in the public mind, Powell is believed to have undermined the understanding of the parties to extricate race from politics. On one level of analysis, this

[13] See e.g. Zig Layton-Henry, *The Politics of Race in Britain*, London, Allen and Unwin, 1984, p. 75.

argument has merit. Powell's activities and speeches did alter public perceptions of inter-party differences on immigration. In only three years the percentage of the electorate perceiving no differences between the parties declined from 53 to 36; after Powell's intervention on race, half of the electorate thought the Conservative party more likely to restrict non-white immigration than Labour (see Table 5.2). Moreover, the considerable support for Powell within the electorate and among Conservative party activists unquestionably pushed the Conservative leadership under Edward Heath closer to Powell's illiberal position.[14]

TABLE 5.2. *Public perceptions of party differences on immigration, 1964–1970 (% of respondents)*

Which party is more likely to keep immigrants out?	1964	1966	1969	1970
(*a*) Conservative	26	26	50	57
(*b*) Labour	19	13	6	4
(*c*) No difference	41	53	36	3
(*d*) Don't know	14	8	8	6
Con.% − Lab.%	+7	+13	+44	+53

Source: David Butler and Donald Stokes, *Political Change in Britain*, 2nd edn., New York, St. Martin's, 1974, table 14.9.

These developments, however, hardly terminated the bi-partisan consensus. First, as we saw in Chapter 2, Conservative leaders publicly distanced themselves from Powell. Indeed, Powell's enormous popularity was primarily a function of his dissenting, anti-establishment posture. Second, the Conservative party leadership did not initially capitalize on its anti-immigrant public image. Like its predecessors, the Heath leadership generally avoided discussing race-related subjects. Third, while the Conservative party moved closer after 1968 to Powell's positions, so did Labour. Thus, Powell's ultimate impact on the racial consensus was not to dissolve it, but to shift it further to the right.[15] And fourth, Powell's intervention

[14] Ibid., pp. 76–7.
[15] Chris Mullard, *Black Britain*, London, Allen and Unwin, 1973, pp. 58–64.

did not inhibit the major parties from co-operating on race-related issues in Parliament. For example, the Conservative front bench did not obstruct Labour's 1976 Race Relations Act despite protests from its right wing.

Indeed, what is striking in retrospect about Powell's overall position in British politics between 1968 and 1974 is how politically isolated Powell was and how similarly both major party leaderships viewed him. By the early 1970s:

Powell stood poised apart from both major parties. He also stood poised on the very peak of his popularity with the public. In the wake of the Ugandan Asian controversy he had actually overtaken Heath in the polls as a popular choice for prime minister and was not far behind Wilson. . . . By June 1973 Powell was in a virtually dead-heat with the two leaders. . . .

He had broken with the major parties on immigration, Northern Ireland, and economic policy, though on all three issues—especially the last—a significant section of Tory opinion sympathized with him.[16]

During this period the parties' consensus on race, like their broader post-war consensus, was eroding. But neither had eroded sufficiently by 1974 to locate Powellism in the political mainstream, even within the Conservative party. As a consequence, Powell found himself as much at odds politically with his own leadership as with Labour's. Even as late as 1976 Powell's views on race were too far outside the bipartisan consensus to be embraced enthusiastically by the Conservative party leadership.

Much of Powell's political orientation, including his racial illiberalism, was eventually adopted by the Conservative party after 1974. As we shall see in Chapter 6, the Conservative leader Margaret Thatcher effectively undermined the bipartisan consensus on race by overtly appealing to racist public sentiment in the late 1970s. However, by then, Powell had broken away from the Conservative party over his policy differences with the leadership. In retreating to Northern Ireland to represent the constituency of South Down in October 1974, Powell removed himself from the forefront of

---

[16] Schoen, op. cit., pp. 115–16.

political opposition to the racial consensus of the major
parties.[17]

The withdrawal of Powell from English politics after 1974
created a political vacuum. On the right, anti-immigrant
public sentiment lost its principal and most powerful voice.
On the left, the departure of Powell to Northern Ireland
created an opportunity to seize the political initiative on race
from the illiberal right, which for years had dominated public
discussion. Eventually filling this void were extra-parliamentary protest movements. Unlike the major parties who failed to
come to grips with race, the National Front and the Anti-Nazi
League offered citizens an opportunity to express their
sentiments and, in the process, register their dissatisfaction
with the parties. While most citizens did not participate
actively in extra-parliamentary groups, tens of thousands
were receptive to the appeals of one or other of these groups,
and implicitly endorsed their opposition to the parties'
consensus on race.

The National Front was primarily, but not exclusively,
founded in response to the neglect of race-related issues by the
parties. As a union of the former British National Party and
the League of Empire Loyalists, the Front inherited the
ideological baggage of anti-Semitism and opposition to
Britain's post-war decolonization, two prominent themes
among far-right political groups in the 1960s.[18] The issue of
race, however, generated the coalition which brought the
National Front to birth as a movement in February 1967.
Despite periodic attempts by the leadership of the Front to
broaden the platform of the movement, race remained the
most salient issue among NF sympathizers. Perhaps 75 per
cent of National Front members initially joined the party as a

[17] Gary P. Freeman, *Immigrant Labor and Racial Conflict in Industrial Societies*,
Princeton, Princeton Univ. Press, 1979, p. 295.
[18] Martin Walker, *The National Front*, Glasgow, Fontana, 1978, pp. 25–67.

result of their dissatisfaction with the course of British immigration policy.[19]

Political opposition to racism, and particularly the fascist brand of racism espoused by the National Front, was principally organized in the 1970s by groups outside the British political mainstream. The most prominent of these groups was the Socialist Workers' Party (SWP) (formerly International Socialists) which in 1966 emerged as an independent political force after attempting unsuccessfully to penetrate the Labour party in the 1950s and early 1960s.[20] The SWP's campaign against the NF was primarily motivated by its perception that the political left had 'abandoned' non-whites and implicitly accepted the arguments of the Front for strict immigration controls. The SWP criticized the reluctance of the major parties to challenge the National Front's illiberal message.

It was the highly publicized electoral advances of the National Front in the 1977 Greater London Council elections, however, which ultimately convinced many left activists, and specifically those within the SWP, to create a broad-based, umbrella movement to combat the Front. As a direct consequence of the Front's modest electoral surge, the Anti-Nazi League was founded in November 1977 at a House of Commons meeting sponsored by the then Labour parliamentary candidate Ernie Roberts, the anti-apartheid campaigner and recent Labour convert Peter Hain, and the prominent SWP activist Paul Holborow. Despite the participation of Roberts, Hain, and several Labour MPs, however, the driving force behind the ANL was the Socialist Workers' Party. The SWP was primarily responsible for monitoring the activities of the National Front and organizing anti-Front demonstrations. Indeed, most of the early initiatives of the ANL were an extension of the SWP's continuing campaign against the National Front. Unlike the major parties, the SWP was not associated with previous efforts to depoliticize race, thus giving the fledgling ANL an unblemished record in this area.

[19] Walter, *The National Front*, p. 58; and Stan Taylor, *The National Front in English Politics*, London, Macmillan, 1982, pp. 100–1.
[20] Taylor, op. cit., p. 32.

The ANL articulated its primary objectives in 1978.[21] They were:

(a) that in the general election Nazi propoganda and activities be actively opposed;

(b) that wherever the Nazis and racialists attempt to organise at local level, there is effective activity by the Anti-Nazi League working with other anti-racist organisations;

(c) that an organisation against the Nazis and racialists in the trade-union movement be set up, involving support from national, regional, districts, and local trade-union bodies, together with a vigorous campaign at rank and file level, on the factory floor, in the office, amongst miners, teachers, engineers, transport workers, printers, etc;

(d) that together with Rock against Racism, SKAN [School kids against Nazis] etc., young people—unemployed, school-students, apprentices and young workers—be organised against the Nazis and racialists;

(e) that we mobilise women through Women Against the Nazis, in co-operation with other groups.

Explicit in these aims was a single, overriding purpose: to erode popular support for the National Front. Absent from the list of potential ANL allies were references to the major political parties and particularly Labour. This omission can primarily be explained by the perception of the founders of the ANL that Labour's parliamentary leaders had avoided race-related issues in the past and therefore could not be trusted: 'The main political parties had attempted to depoliticize race with Labour in particular arguing that the racists could not be taken head on.'[22] The emergence of the League was a response to the unwillingness of Labour to adopt a visible anti-racist profile.

GROWTH AND DEVELOPMENT OF EXTRA-PARLIAMENTARY PROTEST MOVEMENTS

Once protest movements coalesce, their viability and popular support are inextricably linked to the prominence of the issue

[21] 'Leading the Fight Against Fascism and Racism', *Tribune*, 22 Sept. 1978, 19.
[22] Author's interview with Peter Hain, 9 Dec. 1980.

or set of concerns which generated their birth. As long as these issues remain salient and political parties do not address them to the satisfaction of the electorate, protest movements are likely to flourish. Following this pattern, NF support throughout the 1970s ebbed and flowed with the tide of racial tensions and specific racial incidents. According to Taylor:

The importance of the immigration issue [to the National Front] may be illustrated in two ways. Firstly, the NF's membership grew . . . in late 1972 and early 1973 when it won around 11,000 new adherents, and in the spring and summer of 1976, when it gained an additional 5,000 supporters. These major increases . . . follow[ed] government decisions to admit . . . the Ugandan Asians in 1972 and the Malawi Asians in 1976. It is difficult to conceive of reasons other than reaction to these decisions which could explain this pattern of growth in NF membership, or why, at other times, the party's membership fell. Secondly, the theme of immigration and its effects predominated among the various accounts . . . as to why people not previously involved in extreme right politics became NF members.[23]

Front membership probably peaked at 14,000 to 20,000 between late 1972 and early 1974. Opinion surveys taken at the time indicated that over half the public disapproved of the handling of the Ugandan refugee controversy by the government and recommended that the Asians be refused entry into Britain (See Table 5.3).

Moreover, there is evidence that affinity for the National Front among the general public ran deeper. Harrop *et al.* have estimated that approximately 15 per cent of the British public sympathized with the movement. In a poll conducted in 1978, long after the electoral support of the NF had waxed, one-quarter of all respondents agreed that the Front expressed the views of 'ordinary working people' and 21 per cent thought it would be 'good for Britain' if NF candidates gained seats in Parliament.[24] Given the reluctance of all but a small percentage of the electorate to vote for National Front parliamentary candidates, Harrop *et al.* are undoubtedly correct in suggesting that most Front sympathizers viewed the

[23] Taylor, op. cit., pp. 100–1.
[24] Martin Harrop, Judith England, and Christopher T. Husbands, 'The Bases of National Front Support', *Political Studies*, 28.2, June 1980, 271–83.

TABLE 5.3. *Public opinion on the immigration of Ugandan Asians, September 1972 (% of respondents)*

(1) *Do you approve or disapprove of the British Government's handling of the situation of the Ugandan Asians?*

(a)	Approve	28
(b)	Disapprove	54
(c)	Don't know	18

(2) *Do you think that we should or should not let the Ugandan Asians settle in this country?*

(a)	Should	32
(b)	Should not	57
(c)	Don't know	11

Source: The Gallup International Public Opinion Polls, Great Britain, 1937–75, New York, Random House, 1976.

NF as a 'catalyst of change' and not a legitimate party of government. Thus, even overt manifestations of NF sympathies, such as electoral support, were probably motivated by the desire of citizens to 'send the parties a message' on race.

In the early 1970s, the National Front attempted to influence Conservative race policy by infiltrating the party through the Monday Club, a right-wing organization of Conservative party activists. As Walker describes this connection:

The Club was to be a halfway house between the Tories and the NF and this approach was made clear in a major article in the March 1970 *Spearhead*: 'The Monday Club has a useful purpose as a rallying point and recruiting ground for people of patriotic inclinations. It does not serve as a reliable source of guidance for Britain's future.'[25]

The Monday Club was supposed to rally Conservative opposition to non-white immigration and to build grass-roots support for repatriating already settled non-whites. In one of the most visible incidents of co-operation between the National Front and the Monday Club, Club members canvassed for the NF candidate in the 1972 Uxbridge

[25] Walker, op. cit., p. 119. *Spearhead* was the major NF publication at the time.

parliamentary by-election, thus helping the National Front to receive 8.2 per cent of the vote.[26]

Anxious to discredit parliamentary democracy and shy about its Nazi origins, the NF before 1973 was not keen on fighting elections.[27] However, the failure of a Conservative government to restrict all new immigration convinced the NF that its anti-immigrant policies could only gain wider acceptance by the public if it challenged the Conservative party in the electoral arena. After 1972, Edgar suggests, it was impossible for National Front supporters to ignore the gap between the vacillating posture of the Conservative party on immigration and the consistent anti-immigrant line of the NF:

> The Tories' admittance of the Ugandan refugees . . . demonstrated that the state had concluded . . . its restriction of immigration and the continuum had broken. Those racists who had hitherto placed faith in the Tories were rudely awakened. The National Front's own 1968–72 policy of infiltrating the Conservative party, not to gain members so much as to influence grass-roots opinion, was dropped in favour of an open policy of recruitment.[28]

At this juncture, the Front decided to pursue an electoral strategy.

The decision of the Front to contest elections brought mixed results. Apart from the 1973 West Bromwich by-election when it garnered 16.2 per cent of the poll, the party achieved no substantial electoral gains (see Table 5.3). Steed estimates that NF candidates averaged only 3.2 per cent of the vote in 154 general-election contests in 1970 and 1974, while in 25 by-election contests between 1968 and 1978 the average NF vote was a modestly higher 5.2 per cent.[29] The National Front achieved its most impressive electoral results in the 1976 district elections when 80 NF candidates, almost half of the total entered, garnered more than 10 per cent of the poll. As with the surge of Front membership following the Ugandan

[26] Husbands, op. cit., p. 8.

[27] Only 10 NF candidates stood in the 1970 general election. Nationally, the Front put up 45 candidates in the May 1969 municipal elections and 84 in the 1971 local elections, receiving an average 8% and 5.2% of the vote respectively.

[28] David Edgar, 'Racism, Fascism, and the Politics of the National Front', *Race and Class*, 19.2, Autumn 1977, 123.

[29] Michael Steed, 'The National Front Vote', *Parliamentary Affairs*, 31.3, Summer 1978, 284–5.

TABLE 5.4. *National Front: select election results, 1972–1977*

Year	Seats contested	Type of election (mean % of vote)			
		General	By-	District	Metropolitan and county
Oct. 1972	1		8.8		
Dec. 1972	1		8.2		
May 1973	1		16.2		
Nov. 1973	1		3.0		
Feb. 1974	54	3.3			
May 1974	1		11.5		
Oct. 1974	90	3.1			
1975–8	18		4.4		
May 1976	168			8.9	
May 1977	413				4.2

Sources: Michael Steed, 'The National Front Vote', *Parliamentary Affairs*, 31.3, Summer 1978, p. 284; Martin Walker, *The National Front*, Glasgow, Fontana, 1978.

Asian affair, this result too was linked to an increase in racial tensions. The arrival of Asians with British passports who had been expelled from Malawi in the spring of 1976 precipitated an anti-immigrant backlash within the white electorate. Once again, the Front was able to exploit both widespread anti-immigrant sentiment and the dissatisfaction of the public with the major parties.

Indeed, there is evidence that the electoral support of the National Front in the 1970s was primarily a protest vote against the major parties. Using an ecological regression model, Whiteley discovered the best predictor of the National Front vote in the 1977 Greater London Council elections was the Conservative vote, followed by the Labour vote.[30] A reduction of the Conservative vote by 11 per cent increased the National Front vote by 1 per cent of the total; a corresponding reduction of the Labour vote by 12 per cent also raised the National Front's share of the poll 1 per cent. Whiteley's findings challenge the conventional supposition that Front

[30] Paul Whiteley, 'The Decline of Partisan Allegiance in Britain and the National Front Vote', unpublished paper, 1978.

supporters were almost exclusively disaffected Labour sympathizers, an assumption founded on the observation that the National Front historically performed best in safe Labour electoral districts. Rather, Whiteley's regression analysis demonstrates that more Conservative than Labour partisans defected to the NF in the 1977 GLC elections, thus suggesting that *both* parties lost votes to the Front in the late 1970s.

Influencing this equation were, of course, the Liberals, whose electoral support during this period too was mostly a protest vote against the major parties.[31] In their analysis of the general election in February 1974 Butler and Kavanagh argued that the 'main determinant of the NF vote was the presence of a Liberal candidate'. Where there was no Liberal opponent, NF candidates tended to fare better: 'The National Front was most successful where it tapped the protest vote which preferred, if possible, to vote Liberal.'[32]

If the NF vote was predominantly a general protest vote and not specifically linked to race, then our claim that the Front garnered significant electoral support because it alone opposed the major parties' handling of immigration would not be tenable. Therefore, it is relevant that in every constituency where the Front polled well in the October 1974 election a Liberal candidate was present (see Table 5.4). That the Liberals outpolled the NF is not surprising; what is surprising is that the Liberals received only an aggregate 0.3 per cent of the vote more than a neo-Nazi organization. The Front's dent in the Liberal vote in the 1970s is perhaps best evidenced, however, by the 1977 Greater London Council election results; in that election the Front scored third in total votes (119,000) and seats in Inner London, pushing the Liberals into fourth place in 33 of the 92 GLC constituencies.

Moreover, bolstering the argument that the Front's electoral support was primarily a protest vote is the fact that the Front polled better in areas with low voting turnouts. In October 1974 the turnout in National Front electoral strong-

---

[31] For a discussion of this point see Steed, op. cit. For a study of the Liberal attraction of protest votes see Peter Lemieux, 'Political Issues and Liberal Support in the February 1974, British General Election', *Political Studies*, 25.3, Sept. 1980, 323–42.

[32] David Butler and Dennis Kavanagh, *The British General Election of February 1974*, London, Macmillan, 1974, p. 336.

TABLE 5.5. *Constituencies where the National Front polled best, October 1974 (% of electorate)*

Constituency	Total turnout	Party Vote				Labour Majority
		National Front	Liberal	Conservative	Labour	
Hackney, South and Shoreditch	54.7	9.4	11.7	14.9	64.0	49.1
Haringey, Tottenham	56.2	8.3	8.6	24.3	58.8	34.5
Haringey, Wood Green	62.3	8.0	14.8	25.9	51.3	25.4
Newham, South	53.5	7.8	11.7	11.2	69.3	57.6
Tower Hamlets, Bethnal Green and Bow	53.0	7.6	13.0	10.5	68.9	55.9
Newham, North East	59.2	7.0	12.5	22.2	56.9	34.7
Leicester, East	72.3	6.4	12.3	36.5	44.8	8.3
Waltham Forest, Walthamstow	66.2	5.5	15.0	24.3	55.1	30.8
Waltham Forest, Leyton	62.7	5.4	13.4	26.3	54.9	28.6
West Bromwich, West	62.8	5.4	9.6	22.8	62.2	39.4
Islington, Central	55.4	5.3	15.1	21.1	58.5	37.4
Leicester, West	68.4	5.1	11.6	30.4	52.9	22.5
All 90 constituencies contested by National Front	69.6	3.1	16.5	35.0	45.0	10.0
UK Total	72.8	0.4	18.3	35.9	39.3	3.4

Source: The Times Guide to the House of Commons May 1979, London, Times Books, 1979.

holds was significantly lower than the national average of 72.8 per cent, a trend also visible in the 1977 GLC elections. Indeed, Whiteley found turnout to be the third most efficient predictor of National Front support (after the Conservative and Labour shares of the total vote): a decline in turnout of approximately 7 per cent increased the National Front vote by 1 per cent. Interpreting low turnout as a partial measure of political alienation and taking into account the socio-economic attributes of London's constituencies, Whiteley concludes that the National Front vote was predominantly an *alienated, working-class vote.*[33]

The apparent failure of the major parties to undercut the popular support of the National Front facilitated the evolution of the Anti-Nazi League from a paper organization in November 1977 into a mass movement by the summer of 1978. Not since the Campaign for Nuclear Disarmament in the 1960s had an extra-parliamentary organization mobilized such a mass following. Virtually overnight a network of 250 local ANL branches appeared with 40,000 to 50,000 paid-up members. On the strength of mostly small contributions the League raised £600,000 between 1977 and 1980. Despite the absence of a strong central organization the first ANL conference in July 1978 attracted over 800 delegates.

From its founding, the ANL eschewed conventional politics in favour of 'extra-parliamentary action'. The League engaged in three major activities to undermine the popular appeal of the National Front. The most innovative ANL activity was staging carnivals, or political rallies accompanied by popular musical entertainment. The rationale of this strategy was explained by Peter Hain in *Tribune*:

The . . . carnival[s] point the way to the style of campaigning that is likely to win the emerging rearguard battle which must be waged against the National Front. In the longer term, of course, socialist solutions will need to be pressed and fought for. But, in the short term, we desperately need to undercut the support of the new Nazis.[34]

The first full year of these rallies in 1978 was an unqualified success, attracting 30,000 supporters in Manchester and 80,000 and 70,000 in London. The League was especially

---

[33] Whiteley, op., cit.
[34] 22 Sept. 1978, 19.

interested in appealing to young people who, according to several studies, were disproportionately represented within the ranks of the National Front. The carnivals provided the Anti-Nazi League with a platform to influence this constituency.

The second and most controversial of the major activities of the ANL were the demonstrations it sponsored in areas where the NF planned to march or enjoyed influence. Although often planned by the League's national leaders, mobilizing activists for these events was the responsibility of one or more of the ANL's local branches. The tactic of counter-demonstrating hurt the public image of the ANL due to the violence which sometimes accompanied these events. The popular press especially held a negative view of the ANL after 1978.[35] However, from the perspective of the League, counter-marches were essential to its anti-racist initiative. As one ANL founder stressed:

The problem of the National Front and racism can only be defeated by having a large involvement of people. . . . Most of the other anti-racist organizations are fairly moribund. We have emphasized actions rather than committee meetings.[36]

Counter-demonstrations distinguished the ANL from the political parties which it accused of doing little to counter the NF threat. The primary purpose of this activity was to intimidate National Front members.

The third major activity employed by the ANL was disseminating anti-Front propaganda. In its first year of existence the League distributed 5,250,000 leaflets and sold a million anti-NF badges and stickers. This effort was intended to brand the National Front a Nazi organization, a designation ANL leaders thought Britons would find more objectionable than the label 'racist'. ANL leaders conjectured that successfully pinning the Nazi label on the Front would undermine the electoral support of the NF among older voters with memories of Hitler's Germany.

The decision to eschew conventional politics in favour of extra-parliamentary activities did not completely isolate the ANL from the Labour party. In addition to the involvement of several Labour activists in the League's leadership, four

---

[35] See e.g. Gerald Bartlet, 'Anti-Nazi League Members See Themselves as New Crusaders', The *Daily Telegraph*, 26 Apr. 1979, 8.
[36] Quoted in The *Guardian*, 22 Sept. 1978, 13.

Labour MPs initially joined the steering committee of the ANL out of a group of 43 which sponsored the founding statement of the movement in 1977. Several major Labour politicians, including the then Cabinet Minister Tony Benn, addressed audiences at the ANL's massive rallies. However, the unofficial, personal involvement of these Labour MPs made conspicuous the non-involvement in the ANL's campaign of the party's policy-makers on race and immigration and the reluctance of central party headquarters to endorse the League. Although supported by many grass-roots party activists, the ANL failed to ally formally with Labour.

DECLINE OF EXTRA-PARLIAMENTARY FORCES AND THEIR
RELATIONSHIP WITH PARTIES

The electoral support and wider public sympathy for the National Front collapsed just prior to the 1979 general election. Despite offering a record number of candidates, the aggregate number of votes NF candidates received in 1979 increased by little more than one and a half times over that of previous elections (see Table 5.6). In every parliamentary constituency where an NF candidate stood for a second time,

TABLE 5.6. *National Front: general-election results, 1970–1983*

Year	No. of candidates	Total votes	Average vote/candidate	Mean % of vote	Best single consituency result (%)
1970	10	6,000	600	3.6	5.6
1974, Feb.	54	76,865	1423	3.2	7.8
1974, Oct.	90	113,843	1265	3.1	9.5
1979	303	191,706	633	1.4	7.6
1983	60	27,065	451	1.1	3.7

Sources: Michael Steed, 'The National Front Vote', *Parliamentary Affairs*, 31.3, Summer 1978; *The Times Guide to the House of Commons May 1979*, London, Times Books, 1979; David Butler and Dennis Kavanagh, *The British General Election of 1983*, London, Macmillan, 1984.

party support declined. The percentage loss from the previous general election was considerable in many constituencies, plummeting as much as or more than two-thirds in some (see Table 5.7). The average vote per candidate declined by half from 1974 and slumped to the 1970 level of approximately 600 votes per candidate.

TABLE 5.7. *National Front: select constituency results, 1974 and 1979*

Constituency	National Front vote as percentage of total poll		Change
	Oct. 1974	May 1979	
Blackburn	4.4.	1.5	−2.9
Bolton, West	2.7	0.9	−1.8
Enfield, Edmonton	4.6	2.6	−2.0
Leicester, East	6.4	2.7	−3.7
Leicester, South	4.1	1.8	−2.3
Rochdale	4.1	1.4	−2.7
Walsall, South	2.8	1.8	−1.0
West Bromwich, East	4.3	2.9	−1.4
West Bromwich, West	5.4	3.4	−2.0

Source: The Times Guide to the House of Commons May 1979, London, Times Books, 1979.

Within London, the election returns were generally brighter. As in previous elections, the NF enjoyed its greatest success in the East End of London, where it received 7.6, 6.2, and 6.1 per cent of the poll in the respective constituencies of Hackney South and Shoreditch, Newham South, and Tower Hamlets, Bethnal Green and Bow. However, even in these contituencies NF support declined from October 1974. Moreover, the Front failed to gain ground in London constituencies with sizeable ethnic-minority populations and in Haringey, Tottenham suffered an especially sharp and disappointing setback. Overall, NF candidates gained an average share of 2.17 per cent of the vote in the 88 London seats they contested. While higher than the national mean, these results reversed gains made by the Front in the Greater London Council elections only two years earlier.

What accounts for the electoral decline of the Front? Considerable credit must be given to the efforts of the Anti-Nazi League. By making the NF *the* issue in its campaign, the

ANL focused public attention on the National Front in a manner that diminished its appeal as an electoral alternative. The Anti-Nazi League drew the Front out into the open where, for the first time in its history, it became the subject of a widespread political debate. However, the partial appropriation of the National Front's posture on race by the Conservative party (see Chapter 6), a shift precipitated by the election of Margaret Thatcher as party leader in February 1975, was undoubtedly the principal cause of the National Front's poor electoral showing. Thatcher's personal instincts on race, as on several other key issues, were to disavow existing policy consensuses. Her departure from the bipartisan consensus on race was evident in a pre-election interview Thatcher granted to Granada television in January 1978:

If we went on as we are then by the end of this century there would be four million people of the New Commonwealth or Pakistan here.

Now I think that is an awful lot and I think it means that people are rather afraid that this country might be rather swamped by people with a different culture. . . . So if you want good race relations, you have got to allay people's fears on numbers.[37]

Allaying 'people's fears' meant, specifically, that the Conservative party would adopt the National Front's illiberal analysis of the immigrant 'problem'. In the process, Thatcher hoped to appropriate the Front's bread-and-butter issue for her own electoral campaign. That she succeeded was almost immediately evident: Thatcher's remarks concerning the 'swamping' of British culture netted her a 9 per cent gain in the public opinion polls.[38]

Within the NF it was widely held that Thatcher had appropriated the immigration issue, thereby costing the party a substantial number of votes. One prominent Front spokesman cited 'Mrs. Thatcher's apparent anti-immigrant stance' as the principal reason for the NF's poor election results,[39] a view echoed, among others, by Layton-Henry:

It seems clear that the major reason for the electoral reverse was Mrs. Thatcher's public identification of the Conservative party with

[37] Quoted in *The Times*, 31 Jan. 1978.
[38] NOP poll cited in Layton-Henry, op. cit., p. 151.
[39] The newly elected NF chairman Andrew Brons as quoted in, *The Times*, 1 Mar. 1980, 2.

a tough line on immigration. The massive swings to the Conservatives in the ten constituencies stretching from Islington Central through the East End to Dagenham, which averaged 14.2 per cent, were areas where the National Front had achieved some of its highest support and it appears to have lost much of it to the Conservatives.[40]

As a consequence of Thatcher's racial illiberalism, citizens disillusioned with the previous record of the parties on immigration were encouraged that voting Conservative was an effective expression of anti-immigrant sentiment. Unlike past prime-ministerial candidates, Thatcher had addressed herself (however inadequately) to the fears of the electorate about immigration and, for the most rabid racists, vaguely hinted that she might support repatriating non-whites.[41]

At the other end of the political spectrum, the preoccupation of the Anti-Nazi League with the National Front, the key to the meteoric rise of the movement, was responsible for its decline after the NF's electoral support collapsed. Within months after the 1979 general election many of the local branches of the ANL disbanded. Unlike the Front, the decline of the ANL was somewhat voluntary, as its leaders deliberately decreased anti-Front activity.[42] However, like the NF, the future of the ANL was linked to the parties' posture on race in that its survival depended on the continued unwillingness and/or inability of the Labour party to assume an anti-racist posture. As we shall see in Chapter 6, the subsequent adoption of progressive policies on race by Labour—a metamorphosis precipitated by intra-party pressures and the abandonment by the Conservatives of the racial consensus—coupled with the quiescence of the Anti-Nazi League since 1980 highlight our thesis that these extra-parliamentary movements thrived in the context of the parties' neglect of popular concerns on race.[43]

CONCLUSIONS

The failure of the parties to address the race issue in the 1960s

---

[40] Layton Henry, op. cit., p. 106.
[41] *The Times*, 31 Jan. 1978.
[42] Author's interview with Paul Holborow.
[43] Husbands, op. cit., p. 1.; and Taylor, op. cit., p. 173.

and 1970s had important consequences for both citizens and parties;[44] for the parties, the most serious of these was the emergence of extra-parliamentary groups which challenged the legitimacy of their refusal to recognize race as a relevant political subject. Lining up on both the liberal and illiberal side of the race issue and superficially resembling American single-issue interests, these groups differed markedly from their US counterparts in several key respects. Unlike most traditional interest groups, the Anti-Nazi League and the National Front (after 1972) did not in the 1970s attempt to penetrate government. The *raison d'être* of the ANL, as we have seen, was to check the advance of the National Front, a task League organizers claimed that Labour could or would not undertake. Similarly, the Front's scope of concerns, though wider than its opposition to non-white immigration and a multiracial society, primarily centred on its goal to expel or 'repatriate' non-whites. It attempted to facilitate this result by disrupting, often violently, the peace of communities where large numbers of non-whites reside. While the Front did pursue an active electoral strategy after 1973, and made significant electoral inroads in the 1976 district elections, capturing the British political system via elections was never a viable or central strategy of the NF.[45]

Moreover, success for Britain's racist and anti-racist groups was defined primarily in terms of pressures that could be brought to bear on actors outside conventional political institutions. Both groups attempted to shape public attitudes toward ethnic minorities. This strategy bypassed government and presented the case of both proponents and opponents of racism directly to the larger public. Such a course aimed at influencing the social environment in which ethnic minorities live.

Both the popular advances of the Front and the formation of the Anti-Nazi League in the 1970s coincided with widespread citizen dissatisfaction with the stance of the major parties on race.[46] Here, however, cause and effect mix. The

---

[44] Perhaps the most disquieting consequence for citizens was the violence which often erupted when racist and anti-racist groups collided.

[45] Taylor, op. cit., p. 81.

[46] See Ch. 2.

National Front's and the ANL's support were certainly due to the salience of race as a public concern yet, once in existence, these groups mobilized citizens in impressive numbers. Unlike the major parties, which failed to address popular anxieties, both the racist and anti-racist movements offered citizens an opportunity to express their sentiments on race and, in the process, register their dissatisfaction with the parties. On this last score, it is significant that the popularity of both movements can be attributed to what they opposed rather than proposed. For the ANL, the bond uniting its politically diverse supporters was resistance to the Front; for the NF, and its motley group of racists, hostility toward non-whites and non-white immigration. Both movements were nurtured at various times by activists of the major political parties, with the ANL in particular incorporating Labour party activists into its leadership. However, at no point did the major parties offer either organization their official support.

The National Front and the Anti-Nazi League originated and thrived outside conventional political contexts. There is scant evidence that they aspired to supplant the major political parties or assume a long-term role within the British political system as currently constituted. Perhaps the lasting impact of these groups was the voice they allowed citizens who wanted the parties to adopt less ambiguous positions on race. The extent to which the major parties have responded to these pressures since the mid-1970s will be discussed in Chapter 6.

6

The Repoliticization of Race

INTRODUCTION

As antagonists of the racial consensus, the National Front and the Anti-Nazi League exposed and exploited the Conservative and Labour parties' neglect of race-related issues. Both groups attracted support from those within both parties who were critical of the racial consensus and, in the case of the National Front, from thousands of disenchanted voters. Partly in response to the public debate which these groups stimulated, the Conservative and Labour leaderships began disengaging from their consensus on race in the mid–1970s. By the early 1980s, the original understanding of the parties had visibly eroded. As we shall see below, change is evident on three fronts: race has emerged as a partisan, electoral issue; divisions between the Conservative and Labour parties, especially at the level of élite opinion, have visibly widened; and the race-related policies of the 1979–83 and 1983–7 Conservative governments have failed, in contrast to the experience of prior administrations, to attract Opposition support. For the first time since the early 1960s, the major parties in Britain have staked out divergent positions on race and presented their policy differences to the British electorate.

Why, after more than a decade, did the racial consensus erode?[1] As we shall see below, the Conservative and Labour parties diverged on race when changing electoral circumstances coincided with strong pressures from within the two

---

[1] In regard to race-related issues, Donley T. Studlar has argued that political élites have followed rather than led public opinion, 'British Public Opinion, Colour Issues and Enoch Powell: A Longitudinal Analysis', *British Journal of Political Sciences* 4.3, July 1974, 371–81. The opposite argument has been made by Nicholas Deakin, 'The Politics of the Commonwealth Immigration Bill', *The Political Quarterly*, 39.1, Jan.–Mar. 1968, 25–45.

parties to 'push' each party's policy in opposite directions. Moreover, only when electoral considerations and intra-party pressures pushed in a similar policy direction within each party, and in different directions between the parties, did inter-party policy conflict on race occur. Intra-party politics were thus as crucial as inter-party politics in precipitating consensus breakup and policy change. Indeed, opponents of the racial consensus within the parties both accelerated its demise and redefined the pattern of party interaction in this field. The current strength of anti-consensus forces within each party signals the renewal of party competition on race.

THE REPOLITICIZATION OF RACE

(i) The renewal of fundamental party debate

The most obvious evidence that race has re-emerged as a partisan issue is the increasing frequency with which the élites of both parties have addressed themselves to race-related issues since the mid–1970s. This can be seen in the propensity of those responsible for formulating and articulating race-related policies, notably the Prime Minister, Home Secretary, junior Home Office ministers, and their Opposition counterparts to inject these issues into public discussion. Conservative party leaders began to abandon the racial consensus around 1975 when the shadow Home Secretary, William Whitelaw, delivered a series of speeches over an eighteen-month period catapulting race to the forefront of British politics. In an address to the Conservative Party Annual Conference in 1976, Whitelaw declared: 'There will be those voices raised . . . condemning any rational discussion of immigration policies as racist. . . . [However] no one is going to accuse us of any conspiracy of silence.'[2] Fifteen months later, the Conservative leader, Margaret Thatcher, expanded upon his remarks: 'I think there is a feeling that the big political parties have not been talking about this [immigration] and sometimes . . . we are falsely accused of racial

---

[2] Address to the Conservative Party Annual Conference, 5 Oct. 1976.

prejudice. . . . Now we are a big political party. If we do not want people to go to extremes—and I do not—we ourselves must talk about this problem and we must show we are prepared to deal with it.'[3] Thatcher's intervention in this area of public policy was the first time since 1965 that a prime-ministerial candidate had faced the race question directly, a historical break which was not lost on the British electorate. The setting, a televised interview, and the stridency of her additional comments conveyed the clear message that race would no longer be regarded by Conservative leaders as a politically untouchable subject.

The efforts of Conservative party leaders to address the race issue after 1975 were at least partially responsible for the renewed attention paid to this subject by parliamentary candidates during the 1979 general-election campaign, after years of relative neglect. In contrast to February 1974, for example, when only 6 per cent of all Conservative candidates cited immigration as a campaign issue in their election addresses, fully one-quarter mentioned the issue five years later. In the case of Labour: from a mere 2 per cent of prospective MPs establishing race relations as a campaign theme in 1970, this number escalated to 27 per cent in 1979 and 28 per cent in 1983. Although much of the increased political sensitivity of the candidates can be attributed to cues received from party headquarters, especially among Conservatives, there is little question that MPs have opted independently to consider the race issue both during and between election periods. As we shall see below in the examples of the Monday Club and the Labour Party Race Action Group, the prominence of MPs from both parties within race-related pressure groups indicates the active involvement of MPs in this area of public policy.

(ii) The re-emergence of partisan divisions

The renewal of intra-party discussion on race has graphically exposed significant divisions between the parties which are as profound as during any period since the early 1960s. For the Conservatives, opinion on non-white immigration in recent

[3] As quoted in, *The Times*, 31 Jan. 1978.

years has clustered around increasingly restrictive entry policies; within the Labour party, sentiment for revising previous racially discriminatory legislation has garnered considerable support. In line with the principles of Thatcherite *laissez-faire* social policy, the Conservative party of the 1980s has virtually lost all faith in the institutional machinery designed by both major parties to ensure domestic 'racial harmony'. Labour, by contrast, continues to retain confidence in the efficacy of racial buffers as bulwarks against social turmoil.

Evidence of the extent to which these differences within Parliament may have widened is contained in Table 6.1,

TABLE 6.1. *MPs' attitudes on immigration and repatriation,*
1969 and 1982 (%)

1969: *Britain must completely halt all coloured immigration, including dependants, and encourage the repatriation of coloured persons now living here.*

	Agree	Disagree	Don't know
Labour	6	92	2
Conservative	38	56	6

1982: *Are Britain's present immigration statutes too lenient, too restrictive, or reasonably fair and balanced?*

	Too lenient	Too restrictive	Fair
Labour	6	68	25
Conservative	22	8	70

1982: *Do you favour, oppose, or in some circumstances favour, in others oppose, the voluntary repatriation of Britain's non-white residents?*

	Favour	Oppose	Some circumstances
Labour	2	81	17
Conservative	42	26	32

Sources: Robert C. Frasure, 'Constituency Racial Composition and the Attitudes of British MPs', *Comparative Politics*, 3.1, Jan. 1971; Author's questionnaire, 1982.

which contrasts data from Frasure's 1969 questionnaire with results garnered from the author's 1982 survey of MPs' attitudes on race-related issues.[4] There are two problems in comparing the data. Frasure's question as framed in 1969 was in fact two separate questions, and it is not clear to which query MPs responded. The 1982 survey, in contrast, is fairly straightforward and separates the questions Frasure had tied together. Second, the 1969 survey yielded a higher response ratio than that conducted in 1982. None the less, the representativeness of the latter sample makes comparing the two surveys worth while.

As Table 6.1 demonstrates, the opposition of Labour MPs to severe immigration restrictions altered little over time. Just as 6 per cent of the Parliamentary Labour Party favoured ending non-white immigration and repatriating settled immigrants in 1969, so 6 per cent judged Britain's immigration rules too lax in 1982. While a quarter thought the immigration rules reasonably fair in 1982, more than two-thirds believed they were unnecessarily restrictive. Less than a fifth expressed even conditional support for voluntary repatriation.

Conservative MPs, on the other hand, not only widely supported voluntary repatriation in 1982 but, in contrast to 1969, appeared more inclined to do so. Nearly three-quarters favoured repatriation under some circumstances in 1982, with more than 40 per cent supporting it unconditionally. Somewhat surprisingly, over a fifth found Britain's current immigration rules too lenient, despite numerous restrictions implemented between 1971 and 1982 which virtually eliminated primary non-white entry. The remarks of one Conservative backbencher sum up the dissatisfaction of these Members with the status quo:

The real problem is numbers. The British people never wanted a multiracial society. The bitterness is caused because they were never consulted. It was imposed on them by the political establishment.[5]

---

[4] Frasure's data were based on a return rate of 59% for Labour MPs and 51% for Conservatives, 'Constituency Racial Composition and the Attitudes of British MPs', *Comparative Politics*, 3.1, Jan. 1971, 201–10. Our survey elicited an overall response rate of 25% (n = 135), with the major parties almost equally represented.

[5] Written response to author's postal questionnaire.

Although such sentiment has always existed within Conservative parliamentary ranks, it may have increased. From the relatively small group described by Paul Foot as belonging to the 'Goldwater Right' in 1965, the number of Conservative MPs holding strong, illiberal views on race in 1981 was judged by one source within Conservative party Central Office to be as many as 60, an estimate consistent with the findings of our 1982 survey.[6]

Such illiberalism pervades the Conservative party at many levels and, if anything, is strongest at the grass-roots of the party. In a poll of 500 delegates to the 1983 Conservative Annual Conference, for example, 56 per cent felt that Britain's immigration laws were too lenient, 14 per cent advocated the compulsory repatriation of non-whites, and a quarter thought that the 'best' British society would be exclusively white.[7] In a survey of parliamentary candidates conducted by the Commission for Racial Equality in 1983, 19 per cent of Conservative candidates favoured the repatriation of non-whites compared to 0 per cent of Labour candidates.[8] At the very least these findings suggest that the ranks of Conservatives in the House of Commons will continue to be fed in the future by a significant number of racially illiberal Members. Moreover, illiberal, sitting Conservative MPs will continue to be reinforced in their opinions by activist sentiment in their local constituencies.

Policy differences between the parliamentary parties on race are not limited to immigration and repatriation. As Table 6.2 illustrates, they are equally evident in regard to the appropriateness of state intervention in the area of race relations. Whereas Labour MPs supported either reinforcing or more zealously enforcing the 1976 Race Relations Act, a majority of Conservatives advocated repeal or weakening its implementation. Similarly, while 58 per cent of the PLP favoured strengthening the enforcement powers of the Commission for Racial Equality or replacing it with a more

---

[6] Author's interview with Nicholas True, former aide to the Home Secretary, William Whitelaw, 15 Jan. 1981.

[7] Marian Fitzgerald, *Political Parties and Black People*, London, Runnymede Trust, 1984, p. 21.

[8] *Ethnic Minorities and the 1983 General Election*, London, CRE, 1984, p. 23.

TABLE 6.2. *MPs' attitudes on race-related issues, 1982 (%)*

(1) *Should the Race Relations Act (1976) be more or less rigidly enforced, revised and made stronger, left alone, or abolished?*

	Enforced		Revised	Left alone	Abolished	Other
	more	less				
Labour	35	5	52	0	7	2
Conservative	7	16	12	26	36	3

(2) *Should the Commission for Racial Equality be given greater enforcement powers, supported in its current role, replaced by a new, more effective body, or abolished?*

	Strengthened	Supported	Replaced by more effective body	Abolished
Labour	36	39	22	3
Conservative	2	37	10	52

(3) *Does Parliament have a legitimate statutory role to play in improving race relations?*

	Yes	No	In certain circumstances
Labour	95	3	2
Conservative	43	22	35

Source: Author's questionnaire, 1982.

effective organization, more than half of Conservative MPs supported its abolition. This divergence followed from the wider disagreements between the governing and opposition party about the responsibility of Parliament for improving race relations. Labour MPs were much more sympathetic to the view that Parliament ought to legislate in this area.

(iii) Toward adversarial politics

The most tangible evidence that the major parties have adopted a competitive posture on race, however, lies in the Conservatives' assault upon the Commission for Racial Equality and the opposition of the Labour party to the post–1979 Conservative government's discriminatory immigration policies. These developments run contrary to the state of affairs during the racial consensus when both major parties explicitly supported the CRE and other racial buffers and when immigration controls, whether implemented by a Labour or Conservative administration, drew bipartisan support. For the first time since their understanding on race was reached, the major parties have translated their rhetorical differences into divergent actions on race.

Since coming to power in 1979, the Conservative government has diverged from its predecessors in two ways: it has partially withdrawn support of the network of racial buffers it helped to create in the 1960s and 1970s, and it has dropped any pretence of fostering racial equality in favour of the exclusive pursuit of eliminating non-white immigration. Rich observes that under the Conservatives, 'both the CRE and the local CRCs . . . have been left in effective political limbo, neither abolished as some populists on the right have long wished, nor given active support and encouragement as the small liberal wing in the Conservative party have somewhat pessimistically hoped'.[9] The tenor of the relationship between the CRE and the Thatcher governments of 1979–83 and 1983–7 was established early in Thatcher's first term when £1 million was slashed from the Commission budget inherited from Labour, and a freeze imposed on CRE employment levels, despite a 1978 Home Office recommendation that the Commission should employ an additional 96 members of staff. Moreover, under the Conservatives, the CRE has remained relatively underfunded. Against the backdrop of urban riots and the persistence of racial tensions in the 1980s, the CRE's central-government grant has decreased in real

[9] Paul B. Rich, 'Conservative Ideology and Race in Modern British Politics', in, Z. Layton-Henry and P. B. Rich (eds.), *Race, Government and Politics in Britain*, London, Macmillan, 1986, p. 64.

terms since the Conservative party assumed office in 1979 (see Table 6.3). Political tensions between the CRE and the Conservatives were precipitated in 1980 by the Home Secretary's arbitrary dismissal of four of the CRE's five non-white Commissioners and a dispute between the two sides over the Commission's prerogative to investigate the government's immigration procedures. A high-court judgement in October 1980 in the CRE's favour only further poisoned the government's attitude toward the Commission. In a recent demonstration of its contempt for the CRE, the Thatcher government in the summer of 1987 had not responded to a Commission proposal submitted in 1985 to strengthen the 1976 Race Relations Act.[10]

TABLE 6.3. *Home Office grant to the Commission for Racial Equality, 1978–1985*

Year	Grant in £1975*	Increase over previous year (%)	Government
1978	3,400,690		Labour
1979	4,241,462†	24.7	Labour
1979	3,559,133	4.7	Conservative
1980	3,440,587	−3.3	Conservative
1981	3,445,614	0.1	Conservative
1982	3,386,458	−1.7	Conservative
1983	3,379,845	−0.2	Conservative
1984	3,456,069	2.3	Conservative
1985	3,323,012	−3.8	Conservative

* Current figures adjusted according to World Bank GDP deflator.
† Proposed budget.

Source: Commission for Racial Equality, *Annual Reports*, 1979–86, London, CRE.

The Conservatives have further restricted immigration, to the point of virtually eliminating primary non-white entry, by their 1980 and 1983 revision of the immigration rules and the passage of a new British Nationality Act. The 1981 Nationality Act, although ostensibly similar to the Labour Govern-

[10] Claire Sanders, 'A Question of Race', *New Society*, 29 May 1987, 25.

ment's 1977 Green Paper on the subject, nevertheless further limits the potential claims of New Commonwealth residents to British citizenship. It departs from historical precedent in two key respects for non-whites. First, it grants citizenship to children born in the United Kingdom only when an individual can claim a legally settled parent in the country or one currently holding British citizenship; previously, citizenship automatically went to all children born on British soil. Second, it terminates (after a five-year grace period) the automatic citizenship claims of wives of British citizens and Commonwealth residents settled in Britain before 1973, who will be required to apply for naturalization; this process will take up to three years and requires the applicant to be of 'good character' and have 'sufficient knowledge' of English. The new Nationality Act legitimizes recent Conservative alterations of the immigration rules and much of the racially discriminatory immigration legislation enacted since 1962. By raising to £100,000 the capital sum required of foreign businessmen wishing to settle in the country, the 1980 rules showed their bias against non-whites, since a substantial proportion of small investors would be expected to originate from India and East Africa. This racial bias was reinforced in 1986 by the Conservative government's unexpected introduction of visa requirements for visitors from India, Pakistan, Bangladesh, Ghana, and Nigeria.[11]

Both the Conservative government's revisions of the immigration rules and its 1981 Nationality Bill were vehemently opposed in Parliament by Labour. Labour's front bench publicly denounced them as inconsistent with the goal of harmonious race relations. In January 1981 the shadow Home Secretary and, as we saw in Chapter 2, a former leading Centrist, Roy Hattersley, in an address to the Co-ordinating Committee of Pakistani and Kashmiri Organizations, described the pending Nationality Bill as wholly preoccupied with immigration and racially and sexually discriminatory.[12] In October 1981 he pledged that a future Labour government would 'repeal the Nationality Act and . . . replace [it] with a

[11] David Mullins, 'Events and Trends in Race Relations: July–December 1986', *New Community*, 13.3, Spring 1987, 435–6.
[12] Address delivered on 18 Jan. 1981.

definition of British citizenship that does not create second-
class and third-class and fourth-class citizens, that does not
discriminate against ethnic minorities and does not discriminate against women'. In its stead: 'a new Citizenship Bill
introduced by our government . . . [would] . . . restore the
principle that every child born in Britain is automatically
British, without question, without argument, and irrespective
of race and colour'.[13] Hattersley further promised to 'redeem'
the commitment made by previous governments to those East
African Asians wishing to enter Britain who had been
excluded from doing so by the 1968 Immigrants Act. In
acknowledging the validity of this group's claim as British
passport holders, he not only made evident Labour's intention
to reverse the Conservative government's 1979–83 record on
immigration but much of the 1966–70 Labour government's
legislation as well.

   These verbal commitments were reinforced in Labour's
1982 Programme and its 1983 and 1987 election manifestos,
which offered the 'most radical and detailed proposals on
immigration, nationality, and racial equality in the party's
history'.[14] Labour is committed to implementing the following
measures if and when the party returns to office: repeal of the
1981 Nationality Act; repeal of the 1971 Immigration Act;
introduction of 'contract compliance', which will require
businesses which deal with central and local government to
comply with equal opportunity guide-lines; establishment of
an 'independent and balanced' panel of adjudication to hear
immigration appeals; and extension of the investigatory
authority of the Commission for Racial Equality. The
advocacy by Labour of these policies throughout the 1980s
coupled with the explicit endorsement of most of them by the
current Labour leader Neil Kinnock contrasts sharply with
the record of Labour governments and leaders in the 1970s.
As evidence of how far both the major parties have departed
from their racial consensus, Kinnock's outline of Labour's
comparatively liberal immigration policies in a speech
delivered in India in May 1986 prompted the Conservative
Home Secretary, Douglas Hurd, to reply that 'any applause

---

[13] As quoted in, *The Times*, 1 Aug. 1981.
[14] Fitzgerald, op. cit., p. 30.

he may have gained in India will have been dearly bought at home'.[15]

Although much of the movement of the Conservative party on race after 1975 was and is a consequence of the highly partisan, combative style of Thatcher's leadership, there is little question that Conservative headquarters had been under pressure for some time to break the 'rule of silence'. These pressures primarily emanated from two sources: the constituency parties and party-linked pressure groups. While non-white immigration had been a recurrent concern of Conservative local branches since 1961 or so, popular feelings on this issue sharply intensified in the constituencies after 1967 (see Table 6.4). At Conservative Annual Conferences calls for the

TABLE 6.4. *Conservative-conference resolutions on immigration and race relations, 1955–1986*

Years*	Total no. of constituency resolutions on race	Mean resolutions per conference
1955–63	64	8.0
1965–71	194	27.7
1972–9	352	50.3
1980–6	109	15.6

* Party conferences were not held in 1959, 1964, and 1974.

Source: Conservative Conference Agendas, 1955–86.

leadership to speak out and commit itself to ending non-white immigration reached a crescendo in the 1970s, with 200 constituency resolutions on race submitted to the Conservative Party Conference in 1976–7. Representative of the disenchantment of the constituency parties with the national party's relative silence during this period was a resolution proposed by Harborough in 1976: 'In the interests of

[15] As cited in, Marian Fitzgerald, 'Immigration and Race Relations: Political Aspects, No. 16', *New Community*, 13.3, Spring 1987, 442.

immigrants already here as well as ourselves, this Conference calls upon the Conservative leadership to formulate and publicize a clear, firm and essentially restrictive policy on immigration.'[16] Addressing these concerns, Whitelaw pledged in June 1978 that when returned to office his party would 'stabilize' the present and future size of Britain's non-white population by 'ending substantial inflows from any source', thus 'allaying the undoubted fears and anxieties that there is no prospect of an end to the influx of new people from overseas'.[17]

Within Parliament illiberal, anti-immigrant sentiment has principally found voice in the Monday Club, the right-wing pressure group hostile toward the Soviet Union, British participation in the European Community, and non-white immigration. Founded in the early 1960s, its popularity peaked in 1972, when the organization claimed between 4,000 and 6,000 members, 55 affiliated university groups and 34 MPs.[18] Lacking a broad parliamentary base, the Monday Club nevertheless had a disproportionate influence within Conservative circles; the 1970 election victory, for example, swept six Club members into the government. At one time or another such prominent MPs as Cyril Osborne, Geoffrey Rippon, Julian Amery, Sir John Biggs-Davison, Ronald Bell, and Enoch Powell have been among the group's members or political allies. Since its founding, the stance of the Monday Club on non-white immigration has been unambiguous. As a Member of Parliament and Club spokesman put it: 'The Monday Club has held the view for the past twenty years that there should be a complete end to immigration and the repatriation of those who want to take advantage of it.'[19] With its insistence on ending *all* non-white immigration, including dependants of legally settled immigrants, the Club until 1980 remained further to the right on immigration than even the most restriction-minded Conservative government.

In April 1978, however, in a speech reflecting many of the

[16] *Conservative Party Conference Agenda*, London, Conservative Central Office, 1976, p. 90.
[17] Speech to Bow Group, London, 27 June 1980.
[18] Martin Walker, *The National Front*, Glasgow, Fontana, 1978, p. 118.
[19] Author's interview with Harvey Proctor MP, 5 July 1982.

traditional views of the Club, the shadow Home Secretary William Whitelaw proposed measures indicating the 'end of immigration policies based on Britain's past position'. Specifically, he pledged that an incoming Conservative government would:

(a) introduce a new British Nationality Act;
(b) discontinue the practice of allowing permanent settlement for those who came to Britain for a temporary stay;
(c) restrict the entry of parents, grandparents, and children over 18 to those who can prove urgent compassionate grounds;
(d) discontinue the entry concession introduced by Labour in 1974 to husbands and fiancés;
(e) severely restrict conditions under which anyone from overseas can work in Britain;
(f) introduced a register of eligible wives and children from the Indian subcontinent;
(g) introduce an across-the-board quota to control entry;
(h) intensify counter-measures against illegal immigration and overstaying, and help those immigrants who genuinely wish to leave the country.[20]

Taken together, these proposals were the most restrictive posture either major political party had ever adopted on non-white immigration, with points *c*, *d*, and *h* particularly harmonious with the views of the Monday Club. This was no coincidence; at least one Club member and one sympathizer had served on a party panel drafting proposals on immigration policy for the shadow Home Secretary, proposals which Whitelaw incorporated into his 1978 speech.

Unlike the Conservatives, Labour did not easily abandon its strategy of avoiding race-related issues. One might argue that the party has principally reacted to Conservative initiatives, a point substantiated by the slow, unsure manner in which it has dealt with the issue of race since the late 1970s. Like the Conservatives, however, Labour increasingly faced internal pressures throughout the 1970s to speak out on race and adopt clear policies.

[20] Whitelaw in a speech to the Central Council Annual Meeting, Leicester, 7 Apr. 1978.

The principal source of internal pressure for a new strategy was applied by the party's National Executive Committee, whose ideological orientation gradually shifted from right to left in the 1970s. The NEC differed from Labour's traditional posture on race in two ways: it failed to appreciate the political expediency of avoiding the subject; and it fundamentally opposed the party's past support of discriminatory immigration measures. The NEC underscored this second point in its report to the Annual Conference in 1977 during a period of Labour government:

It is greatly to be regretted that the government appears no longer to expect, within the lifetime of this Parliament, to repeal the Tories' racially discriminatory 1971 Immigration Act. Yet there is no doubt that the discriminatory nature of Britain's immigration policy has had an adverse effect on race relations. . . .

We think it is right to remind the party of our commitment in Labour's Programme 1976. 'Immigration needs to be planned and regulated but citizenship and immigration law and administration must not be based on race'. In this context we are disappointed with the [Labour] government's Green Paper on British Nationality Law.[21]

Reiterating its opposition to the legislative record of previous Tory and Labour governments, the NEC argued further in 1980:

Socialists are right to be angry at our British system of immigration control: in its present form it is unjust. . . . But Britain's controls are bad not simply because they are controls: they are seen to be bad in comparison with the fairer practices of other countries. . . .

The next Labour government must repeal the Tory immigration legislation, but it must do much more. It must enact fundamentally different legislation which takes the racist dimension both from the law and from the context of the debate which has until now pervaded our thinking on immigration and nationality.[22]

Between 1978 and 1981 the NEC published no fewer than six documents specifically dealing with race relations and non-white immigration, nearly all of which were highly critical of the earlier consensual approach. These efforts substantially

---

[21] *Statements to the Annual Conference*, London, NEC, Oct. 1977.
[22] Labour National Executive Committee, 'Citizenship and Immigration', London, 1980.

increased the visibility of race-related issues both within and outside the Labour party.

Increasing the public visibility of race-related issues and placing these issues on the national political agenda were two of the three major tasks the Labour Party Race Action Group undertook during its formative years in the 1970s. The third, persuading a majority of the Labour movement to accept 'socialist' policies on race, endures as the long-term objective of the group. The LPRAG was created by a small cadre of Labour activists in 1974 to act as a national and local pressure group. By 1981 it enjoyed the support of 120 constituency Labour parties, and approximately 60 MPs. Included among its early parliamentary supporters were former LPRAG chairpersons Shirley Williams, Alex Lyon, and Labour's former front-bench spokesman on race and immigration, John Tilley.

Like the Monday Club, the Labour Party Race Action Group advocated throughout the 1970s that the bipartisan consensus on race be terminated, criticizing Labour's administrative record on race as one of 'benign neglect' and 'tempered by a reluctance to alienate white supporters'. Also like the Club it was unambiguous on the question of non-white immigration. In an attack on the Conservative government's 1980 White Paper on nationality law, LPRAG offered the following critique of Labour's past immigration policies:

Black people need convincing that there has been a real change of heart since the Labour Governments which introduced the 1968 Commonwealth Immigrants Act and which failed to honour the party's manifesto pledge to repeal the 1971 Act. . . . *The Labour party must oppose the White Paper by reversing the pattern of its own involvement in racist immigration legislation.*[23]

Since 1974 the LPRAG has attempted to redefine Labour policy on race by drafting an alternative strategy and by penetrating the party's relevant policy-making committees. In the latter respect the group has been successful: in 1980, for example, no fewer than nine LPRAG members were represented on Labour's Human Rights and Race Relations Sub-Committee, including five MPs and the group's public

[23] Labour Race Action Group Newsletter, Sept. 1980.

spokesperson. A former chairperson of the Labour Party Race Action Group, Keith Vaz, was one of four ethnic-minority parliamentary candidates elected to the House of Commons in 1987.

Efforts by Labour's National Executive Committee and the LPRAG to move the party away from its reluctance to address the race issue bore modest fruit in 1981 with the appointment of Roy Hattersley, formerly a Centrist on race (see Chapter 2), as shadow Home Secretary and John Tilley as chief parliamentary spokesman on race and immigration. In addition to being more liberal than their immediate predecessors, both men quickly evinced a predilection for speaking out on race and advocating progressive policies. Within months, for example, Hattersley called for positive discrimination in the work-place, a position which would have been difficult for Labour to promote actively only a few years earlier:

> I . . . call for a legal obligation to be placed on employers to use their best endeavours to ensure that the ethnic minorities are properly represented in every workforce, signed on when there are vacancies and promoted. I do not pretend that positive discrimination will be popular, but it is right and it is necessary to the peace and prosperity of the whole community.[24]

Addressing himself to the body which had been in the forefront of the opposition to the racial consensus, Hattersley argued:

> The national executive continually tells us that unpopular policies can be converted into election winners by passionate moral advocacy. I hope they are prepared to evangelize for a fairer employment deal for the ethnic minorities. If they are not, there are others who are prepared to fight on their behalf.[25]

Hattersley's advocacy of what he accurately described as an unpopular position appeared to signal a subtle but tangible break with the past. Indeed, not since the tenure of Roy Jenkins in the late 1960s had a Labour Home Secretary or shadow minister explicitly committed his party to such concrete and progressive race relations policies.[26]

Hattersley's advocacy of positive discrimination in favour of ethnic minorities in employment complemented the Labour

---

[24] *The Times*, 1 Aug. 1981.   [25] Ibid.
[26] For an analysis of Jenkin's tenure as Home Secretary see E. J. B. Rose and Associates, *Colour and Citizenship*, London, IRR/OUP, 1969, pp. 511–50.

party's new, more liberal stance on immigration. As John Tilley described Labour's metamorphosis on immigration:

Passing the 1968 Immigrants Act was wrong in principle and a tactical mistake. The 1974–9 Labour government did not repeal the objectionable parts of the 1971 Immigration Act. [However] there will be a change in race policy . . . The message of the Labour Race Action Group is getting across. It's difficult to tell what kind of support there is for more liberal race policies within the Parliamentary Labour Party . . . [but] a Labour Home Secretary would not be able to get the 1968 Act through the PLP now.[27]

Although untested by the experience of government, Tilley's remarks, in conjunction with recent party-conference decisions and NEC statements, demonstrate considerable agreement within Labour for a more progressive posture on race.[28]

EXTERNAL PRESSURES FOR CHANGE

While Thatcher's personal distaste for consensus politics and internal pressure from the Monday Club and the constituency parties were critical stimuli, electoral considerations undoubtedly played an important role in the Conservative party's movement on race. How central that role was is hard to determine since the motivations of the Conservative leadership during this time are difficult to investigate. However, certain facts are clear. First, both private and published opinion polls in the mid–1970s indicated the electoral gains to be had if the party adopted an explicit, hard line on race.[29] Such gains would have been especially welcome given the near-even popular support of the major parties at the time. Moreover, there is reason to believe that Conservative leaders were concerned about losing some electoral support to the National Front, especially in certain constituencies in the Midlands. When asked in January 1978 whether she hoped to woo Tory defectors to the National Front back to the Conservative party Thatcher replied:

[27] Author's interview, Jan. 1981.
[28] See e.g. 'Opposition Parties and Race Policies, 1979–83', in, Layton-Henry and Rich (eds.), op. cit., pp. 100–14.
[29] See Stan Taylor, *The National Front in English Politics*, London, Macmillan, 1982, p. 147; and Zig Layton-Henry, *The Politics of Race in Britain*, London, Allen and Unwin, 1984, p. 150.

Oh, very much back, certainly, but I think that the National Front has, in fact, attracted more people from Labour voters than from us; but never be afraid to tackle something which people are worried about. We are not in politics to ignore people's worries: we are in politics to deal with them.[30]

From 1977 to 1978 Thatcher's and Whitelaw's public remarks on race were peppered with attacks on the National Front, references which are difficult to explain in the light of the Conservative leadership's indifference to it before this period and since. Thatcher's reference to the 'swamping' of British culture by immigrants on television in 1978 was, as her related comments during the interview clearly demonstrated, a transparent effort to appropriate the National Front's main electoral issue for the Conservative cause.

The rightward drift of the Conservative party on race after 1975 was facilitated by the political eclipse or generational replacement of those most responsible for the bipartisan consensus on race. Gone forever is that segment of the party, especially within Parliament, that had lived, worked, or governed in Britain's former colonies and whose opposition had moderated the Conservative party's movement toward exclusionary entry policies. By 1981 only nine Conservative MPs remained in the House of Commons of the rebellious faction which had voted against Labour's 1968 Commonwealth Immigrants Act. Moreover, as Britain's emotional ties to and trading relationship with its New Commonwealth have declined in favour of Europe, so, too, has support within the Conservative party for a relatively 'open' immigration policy virtually dissipated. This shift in the balance of parliamentary opinion is reflected in the increased number of Conservative MPs since the late 1960s who favour not only the cessation of non-white immigration, but the voluntary repatriation of Britain's non-whites.

Labour's shift in the 1980s toward a comparatively liberal race policy, as virtually all relevant surveys indicate, has cut against the grain of majority public opinion. Unlike the Conservatives, the abandonment of the bipartisan consensus by Labour is as likely to have lost as gained the party electoral support, especially within the white working class where anti-immigrant sentiment prevails. Despite its aggregate vote-losing potential, however, Labour's recent adoption of a liberal posture on race can be seen as electorally motivated. Its principal target is the growing pool of ethnic-minority voters.

The perceived importance of the non-white vote in the late 1970s contributed to fostering consensus within the party for a liberal line on race. This new agreement was influenced by four developments: the rapid expansion of the non-white electorate;[31] the reported high turnout rate of non-white voters;[32] the propensity of non-whites to support Labour (see Table 6.5); and the geographical concentration of ethnic minorities in electorally marginal areas (see Table 6.6). While the practical significance of these developments has been a matter of some controversy among scholars, Labour élites could only conclude, on the basis of the evidence available in the 1970s, that the ethnic-minority vote was important.[33] The findings of the Community Relations Commission in 1975 that the non-white electorate helped put Labour in government in October 1974 were widely publicized and generally accepted as valid.[34] In 1983 the Runnymede Trust identified the existence of 37 'ethnic marginal' parliamentary constituencies where the ethnic-minority vote could decide the local result.[35]

If Labour commanded the overwhelming allegiance of the non-white electorate, why did it risk any white votes? Why did it not continue its traditional tack of wooing non-white voters while simultaneously appeasing anti-immigrant sentiment, a two-track strategy which succeeded fairly well for most of the 1960s and 1970s? This approach was successful only as long as the Conservatives adhered to the bipartisan consensus to depoliticize race and the non-white vote was secure. By the mid–1970s, these conditions could no longer be assumed. The movement of the Conservative party toward an explicit anti-

[31] Non-white voters comprise approximately 2.7% of the total electorate. See Ch. 7.

[32] On this point see Muhammad Anwar, *Votes and Policies*, London, CRE, 1980.

[33] See e.g. Ian McAllister and Donley T. Studlar, 'The Electoral Geography of Immigrant Groups in Britain', *Electoral Studies*, 3.2, Aug. 1984, 139–50; and the Labour party, 'Black People and the Labour Party', London, 1984.

[34] *Participation of Ethnic Minorities in the General Election October, 1974*, London, Community Relations Commission, 1975.

[35] Marian Fitzgerald, 'Ethnic Minorities and the 1983 General Election', Runnymede Trust Briefing Paper, London, May 1983.

The Repoliticization of Race

TABLE 6.5. Non-white voting patterns at general elections, October 1974, 1979, and 1983 (% of vote)

	1974			1979			1983		
	Asian	Afro-Caribbean	Total electorate	Asian	Afro-Caribbean	Total electorate	Asian	Afro-Caribbean	Total electorate
Conservative	n/a	n/a	36	8	5	44	6	8	42
Labour	78	89	39	86	90	37	80	86	28
Liberal/SDP	n/a	n/a	18	5	3	14	12	5	25
Other	n/a	n/a	7	1	2	5	1	2	5

Sources: Muhammad Anwar, Votes and Policies, London, CRE, 1980, pp. 43–50; Ethnic Minorities and the 1983 General Election, London, CRE, 1984, p. 1.

TABLE 6.6. *Constituencies with majorities at three successive general elections smaller than the number of New Commonwealth residents*

	1974 (Feb.)	1974 (Oct.)	1979
Labour	29	35	24
Conservative	12	6	17

Source: Muhammad Anwar, *Votes and Policies*, London, CRE, 1980, pp. 47–8.

immigrant posture meant that Labour could hardly outflank the Conservatives on immigration in a way that could satisfy anti-immigrant sentiment. Accordingly, it was better served by staking out a position to the left of its Conservative opponent. This made it all the more important to keep the active support of ethnic-minority voters. As Labour's National Executive Committee warned in 1980: 'In spite of the party's long standing commitment to anti-racism we have so far failed to convince black people that we deserve their active support. Instead, they have increasingly been organizing politically into self-help and pressure groups, largely spurning mainstream party politics. Indeed, many black people—especially the youngest members of the community—are openly suspicious of the party.'[36] Fearful that a small erosion in its non-white support could have a disproportionately negative electoral impact, Labour closed ranks around progressive policies on race-related issues. In so doing, it appeared to heed the pragmatic message of the Labour Party Race Action Group: 'don't take black votes for granted'.

CONCLUSIONS

As the central thrust of the major parties' consensus through the mid–1970s was the depoliticization of race-related issues, so, after 1975, did the breakup of their 'understanding' lead to the renewal of race as a partisan issue. Why the Conservative and Labour parties diverged after 1975 is fairly clear. Impelled by distinct internal pressures and attempting to woo different electoral constituencies, each side gravitated toward race policies which offered the best prospect for internal

[36] 'Labour and the Black Electorate', Advice Note, Feb. 1980.

political coherence and electoral advantage. For Conservatives, the pull toward an illiberal, anti-immigrant posture was facilitated by the support of this stance among a majority of Conservative MPs and their newly elected leader, Margaret Thatcher. For Labour, the liberal inclinations of its National Executive Committee and the efforts of the Labour Party Race Action Group influenced the party to adopt progressive policies on race, policies which often repudiated its past record. For both parties, the old racial consensus had outlived its utility, primarily because the political conditions under which it was forged in the 1960s had substantially altered. By 1979 the eclipse of the Conservative party's liberal wing on race and Labour's interest in securing the non-white vote induced each party to recast its race policies in the light of these changed political circumstances.

The breakup of the racial consensus was not an autonomous or isolated development. It paralleled the wider disintegration of the parties' post-war consensus which, for the better part of two decades, depoliticized substantial areas of British political life. Just as the spirit of Butskellism encouraged the parties to reach an accommodation on race, so too its decline allowed the renewal of partisan conflict. This was so because the changes wrought by the demise of the parties' larger accord—namely the realignment of the respective leaderships of the parties and the radicalization of partisan conflict—profoundly altered both the style and substance of British politics in a manner which made consensus, of any kind, difficult to sustain.[37]

The apparent absence of overt partisan conflict did not mean, of course, that there were no differences between the parties on race between 1964 and 1975. On the contrary, as we have attempted to show, it was precisely the persistence of these differences—albeit beneath the surface of electoral politics—which eventually guided the parties into an adversarial posture in the late 1970s and early 1980s. Like other issues which were effectively depoliticized during the heyday of the bipartisan era, race regained its former place as a partisan issue because of the very different constituencies

[37] See Dennis Kavanagh, 'Whatever Happened to Consensus Politics?', *Political Studies*, 33.4, Dec. 1985, 529–46.

within each party and the divergence in the long-term electoral interests of the major parties. Not surprisingly, the breakup of consensus has brought the parties very close to the positions they held on race before 1965. As in the earlier period of 'fundamental debate', each party has staked out coherent policies on race-related issues which share little with those of its political opponent.

7

Labour's Non-White Constituency

INTRODUCTION

The renewal of party competition on race, in addition to dividing the Conservative and Labour parties on race-related public policy, has coincided with and precipitated other political change. Specifically, the illiberal record of the Conservative party on race-related issues has reinforced its anti-immigrant public image, while the policies of Labour have further established it as the 'natural' representative of racially liberal opinion.[1] These core party identities are not seamless. Each major party leadership has periodically courted liberal and illiberal racial sentiment during the 1980s.[2] Moreover, although discredited, the Tory Radicals are far from dead.[3] Labour's racially right-wing minority remains sympathetic to the illiberalism of its Conservative counterpart. Yet, for the most part, the political influence of these internal-party factions has waned considerably. The erosion of the racial consensus has undermined their influence on the race policies of the major parties.

As with the disintegration of most policy consensuses, the breakup of the Conservative and Labour parties' understanding on race has yielded political winners as well as losers. Perhaps the chief beneficiary of renewed party competition has been Labour's non-white constituency. The political

[1] Labour has been consistently identified as the party 'particularly good at improving race relations' and the Conservative party as the party most likely to restrict non-white immigration. See *Gallup Political Index* 1978–86, London, Social Surveys (Gallup Poll) Limited.

[2] The Conservative party's campaign to court non-white voters during the 1983 general-election campaign is a case in point. See Zig Layton-Henry, *The Politics of Race in Britain*, London, Allen and Unwin, 1984, p. xv.

[3] See e.g. the Tory Reform Group publication, *Young, British and Black*, London, 1982.

advantages gained by non-whites as a consequence of Labour's commitment to implement less restrictive immigration rules, non-discriminatory nationality statutes, and equal-opportunity employment policies are clear and require little further comment. Two less obvious consequences of party competition, greater non-white voice within Labour and the political mobilization of Labour's ethnic-minority activists, will be analysed in this chapter. As we will argue below, these developments are not necessarily permanent. Nor will they inevitably result in concrete policies favourable to ethnic minorities, even in the unlikely event that Labour returns soon to government. However, in the short term, the relative position of non-whites in Britain's political market has visibly improved. Ethnic minorities have gained, at least temporarily, influence, if modest, over Labour élite politics.

LABOUR'S NON-WHITE VOTERS

Despite the claims of some analysts that a significant non-white 'floating vote' exists and recurrent predictions that the *embourgeoisement* of the Asian community is moving it closer to political conservatism, two facts about the political orientation of non-whites are irrefutable: Asian and Afro-Caribbean electors constitute a solid voting bloc; and these constituencies are extremely loyal to Labour.[4] By virtually all indices, Labour is the party of, if not unambiguously for, non-whites. Among demographic groups in the electorate, non-whites remain among Labour's staunchest supporters.[5]

The propensity of non-whites to vote Labour in local and general elections is well documented. Even if the Commission for Racial Equality's figure of more than 80 per cent is an overestimate (see Table 6.5), other studies have consistently verified that non-whites prefer Labour to its principal

[4] See Ivor Crewe, 'Representation and Ethnic Minorities in Britain', in, Nathan Glazer and Ken Young (eds.), *Ethnic Pluralism and Public Policy*, London, Heinemann, 1983, pp. 258–84.
[5] Ivor Crewe, 'The Disturbing Truth Behind Labour's Rout', *The Guardian*, 13 June 1983.

electoral opponent by a margin of more than two to one (see Table 7.1).[6]

TABLE 7.1. *Non-white voting intentions, 1983 and 1987 (% of respondents)*

	Asians		Afro-Caribbeans	
	1983	1987	1983	1987
Conservative	9	23	7	6
Labour	81	67	88	86
Alliance	9	10	5	7

Source: Harris polls as reproduced in the *Guardian*, 19 June 1987.

Moreover, the non-white vote is very likely a specific ethnic vote; social class does not affect the preferences of non-white voters to nearly the same extent it influences the choices of white voters.[7] Asian routine non-manual (C1) voters excepted, all social classes within the non-white electorate supported Labour by a ratio of more than three to one over other political parties in the 1983 general election (see Table 7.2). In the 1987 general election no social class gave Labour

TABLE 7.2. *Non-white voting intentions by socio-economic group, 1983 (% of respondents)*

Class	Asians			Afro-Caribbeans		
	Conservative	Labour	Alliance	Conservative	Labour	Alliance
AB	0	80	20	0	80	20
C1	30	59	11	4	89	7
C2	12	79	9	4	90	6
D	2	90	8	7	90	3
E	2	94	4	7	92	1

Source: *Black on Black/Eastern Eye*, London Weekend Television, as reproduced in Monica Charlot, 'The Ethnic Minorities' Vote', in Austin Ranney (ed.), *Britain at the Polls, 1983*, Durham, NC, AEI/Duke Univ. Press, 1985, p. 149.

[6] See, e.g. Zig Layton-Henry and Donley T. Studlar, 'The Political Participation of Black and Asian Britons: Integration or Alienation?', *Parliamentary Affairs*, 38.3, Summer 1985, 307–18.
[7] Crewe, 'Representation and Ethnic Minorities', p. 272.

less than 52 per cent or the Conservative party more than 33 per cent of the vote (see Table 7.3). Within the lowest occupational grades (D, E), 9 out of 10 non-white electors in 1983 and more than 8 out of 10 in 1987 voted Labour. These

TABLE 7.3. *Aggregate non-white voting intentions by socio-economic group, 1987 (% of respondents)*

Class	Conservative	Labour	Alliance	other
AB	33	54	13	0
C1	30	52	17	1
C2	14	78	9	0
DE	10	84	5	1

Source: *Harris Research Survey*, 25–9 May 1987, Harris Research Centre.

results generally reinforce the findings of a 1978 NOP survey of ethnic-minority voting preferences. In 1978 middle-class (A, B, C) ethnic-minority voters divided 86 : 14 in Labour's favour in contrast to a 26 : 74 Labour split among middle-class whites.[8]

Sex and age also appear not to influence significantly the attachment of ethnic minorities to the Labour party. In contrast to the partisan divide between the genders within the general British electorate, non-white men support Labour in approximately the same percentage as ethnic-minority women. Moreover, ethnic-minority voters do not necessarily become more politically conservative with age.[9] First-time Asian voters in 1983 and 1987 were somewhat less inclined to vote Labour than the 1979 cohort, but overall 73 per cent of new non-white voters supported the party in each of the last two general elections.[10]

Almost as important as the propensity of non-whites in the aggregate to support Labour is the partisan loyalty that individual voters demonstrate over time. Using a CRE survey of 564 non-whites who recalled their October 1974 vote and who intended to support one of the major parties in the 1979

[8] Ibid., p. 271.
[9] Monica Charlot, 'The Ethnic Minorities' Vote', in, Austin Ranney (ed.), *Britain at the Polls, 1983*, Durham, NC, AEI/Duke Univ. Press, 1985, p. 149.
[10] Ibid.

general election, Taylor discovered that over 90 per cent of 1974 Labour supporters remained faithful five years later.[11] In a 1983 Harris pre-election survey, 76 per cent of Asians and 61 per cent of Afro-Caribbeans claimed to support one political party consistently and, among these respondents, 89 per cent were Labour-inclined.[12] Given this voting pattern, it is improbable that non-white Labour partisans will soon defect in significant numbers to other political parties or, in the event that significant defections occur, that these defectors will desert Labour permanently. Afro-Caribbeans are especially unlikely to defect given the strong working-class identity of this group, which reinforces its attachment to the Labour party.[13]

Despite the cohesion of the ethnic-minority vote, however, many observers have argued that non-whites enjoy inadequate political voice at the national level. We define this political voice as the ability of non-whites, either collectively or individually, to articulate their unique interests, that is to be heard or represented, in the political market-place.[14] Working against the expression of ethnic-minority political voice, it has been postulated, are four unavoidable realities. Non-whites comprise a small percentage of the total national electorate and in few parliamentary constituencies do they hold the electoral balance; moreover, they do not always turn out to vote in high percentages, and are not intensely interested in conventional political affairs and activities. The first two points might be termed 'structural' and the other two 'subjective' obstacles to political influence. Obviously only the subjective barriers can be surmounted fairly easily. This fact has led most scholars to conclude that non-whites are unlikely in the short or long-term to make an impact on British national politics.[15]

These arguments obviously have merit. Non-whites, indeed, comprise little more than 4 per cent of the British

---

[11] Stan Taylor, 'Is the Ethnic Vote a Floating Vote?', *New Community*, 9.2, Autumn 1981, pp. 278–81.
[12] Layton-Henry and Studlar, op. cit., p. 311.
[13] Ibid.
[14] Albert O. Hirschman, *Exit, Voice, and Loyalty*, Cambridge, Mass., Harvard Univ. Press, 1970, p. 30.
[15] Crewe, 'Representation and Ethnic Minorities', p. 279.

population (see Table 7.4) and potential ethnic-minority voters less than 3 per cent of the total electorate. Moreover, these percentages are unlikely to rise appreciably in the near

TABLE 7.4. *Estimated population of New Commonwealth and Pakistani origin in Great Britain, 1951–1981*

Year	New Commonwealth and Pakistani population	% of total population
1951	200,000	0.4
1966	886,000	1.7
1969	1,190,000	2.2
1971	1,371,000	2.5
1974	1,615,000	3.0
1976	1,771,000	3.3
1978	1,920,000	3.5
1981	2,176,000	4.0

Sources: The Runnymede Trust and Radical Statistics Group, *Britain's Black Population*, London, Heinemann, 1980, pp. 1,7; Zig Layton-Henry and Donley T. Studlar, 'The Political Participation of Black and Asian Britons', working paper No. 36, University of Warwick, Feb. 1984, 3.

future. On *ceteris paribus* assumptions, Crewe estimates that by the year 2000 only one in twenty-five British voters will be non-white.[16]

Even a modest expansion of the potential ethnic-minority electorate will, of course, have no political impact if non-whites do not register and turn out to vote in relatively high percentages. On both these scores the historical record up to the mid–1980s is mixed. Until the 1970s non-white electoral registration, especially among Afro-Caribbeans, was low by white British standards. Between a quarter and a half of non-whites may not have been registered.[17] Voting turnout, on the other hand, was probably higher. In some parliamentary constituencies during the 1970s, Asian turnout is estimated to have equalled or exceeded that of whites; in a handful, the non-white vote was nearly fully mobilized.[18] Contrary to these

[16] Ibid., p. 259.
[17] Ibid., p. 269.
[18] Muhammad Anwar, *Votes and Policies*, London, CRE, 1980, p. 38.

earlier trends, over 80 per cent of Afro-Caribbeans and 90 per cent of Asians were reported registered before the 1983 general election. Yet, among those registered, only 68 per cent of Asians and 61 per cent of Afro-Caribbeans may have actually voted.[19] Lower electoral turnout among non-whites thus may be offsetting higher levels of electoral registration.

Voting turnout rates, one expects, would be linked to the interest non-whites evince in general political affairs. It is reasonable to assume that political apathy among non-whites would depress all forms of political activism, including voting. Apathy may have had this impact in the past, but this no longer appears to be the case. Rather, lack of interest in electoral outcomes and politics generally does not necessarily deter non-whites from voting; and, recent evidence suggests that, on the whole, non-whites are only slightly less politically aware than the larger electorate.[20] However, there are differences of political orientation within the non-white community. A Harris poll conducted in May 1987 found Afro-Caribbeans much more dissatisfied than Asians with the race and immigration records of the three main political parties: a fifth of this constituency were dissatisfied with Labour, three-quarters disillusioned with the Conservative party, and more than a quarter unhappy with the Alliance.[21] According to the findings of Layton-Henry and Studlar, Afro-Caribbeans are more inclined than Asians to engage in spontaneous political discussion and organized political activity but they are less inclined to vote.[22] These differences and other evidence have led Layton-Henry and Studlar to conclude that Afro-Caribbeans are 'more frustrated and less satisfied with their experiences in Britain than Asians'.[23] If true, Afro-Caribbeans are probably more likely than Asians to pursue their grievances aggressively and, given their stronger attachments to Labour, to use that party more intensely as a vehicle of political expression. Indeed, there are indications that this may be the case.[24]

[19] Charlot, op. cit., p. 147.
[20] Layton-Henry and Studlar, op. cit., pp. 311–22.
[21] *Harris Research Survey*, 25–9 May 1987, Richmond, Harris Research Centre.
[22] Ibid., pp. 312–13.
[23] Ibid., p. 316.
[24] The initiative for black sections in the Labour party, for example, appears to be dominated by Afro-Caribbean activists.

Many scholars have argued that whatever their aggregate numbers, voting turnout rates, and levels of political awareness and activism, non-whites will never gain significant political representation under Britain's current electoral arrangements.[25] The first-past-the-post electoral system, it has been claimed, penalizes all but the most regionally concentrated electoral minorities and produces too few 'ethnic-marginal' parliamentary constituencies to facilitate non-white political voice.[26] To a considerable extent, these arguments are valid. The tendency of Britain's electoral system to under-represent even large minorities is well known.[27] Also, despite previous claims to the contrary by the CRE, there are in fact only a handful of genuine ethnic marginals. According to Layton-Henry's rigorous estimates, there were 14 in the 1983 general election. Of these, six were defended by Conservative candidates and, to the disappointment of Labour, each was successfully held.[28] However, does the small number of ethnic-marginal constituencies produced by the first-past-the-post electoral system impede the political representation of non-whites as seriously as most analysts assume? Specifically, would the emergence of 20 or 30 ethnic marginals significantly advance the political interests of non-whites?

A two- or threefold increase in the number of ethnic marginals could have a potentially significant political impact under a very special set of conditions:

(*a*)   if a significant percentage of the ethnic minority vote could be electorally and ideologically detached from Labour. The emergence of a substantial number of ethnic marginals would not give non-whites significant political leverage unless, and until, a large percentage of the ethnic-minority electorate in these

---

[25] See John Curtice, 'Proportional Representation and Britain's Ethnic Minorities', *Contemporary Affairs Briefing*, 6.2, London, Centre for Contemporary Studies, Feb. 1983.

[26] Ethnic marginals may be defined as 'marginal constituencies in which the percentage of non-whites is sufficiently large to give one party victory if a large portion of the non-white voters cast their ballots in a particular direction'. Donley T. Studlar, 'The Ethnic Minority Vote, 1983: Problems of Analysis and Interpretation', *New Community*, 11.2, Autumn–Winter 1983, 92.

[27] David Butler, 'Variants of the Westminster Model', in, Vernon Bogdanor and David Butler (eds.), *Democracy and Elections*, London, CUP, 1983, pp. 46–9.

[28] Studlar, op. cit., pp. 92–3.

marginal constituencies was prepared to vote Conservative;[29]

(b)   if both major parties were ideologically free to advance
the interests of non-whites. The willingness of many
non-white voters to float between the major parties
would probably produce little in the way of concrete
policy results if only one party could respond to the
unique demands of these voters (See Chapter 4);[30]

(c)   if the ethnic marginals constituted a large percentage
of all marginal constituencies in circumstances of
virtual electoral parity between the major parties. An
increase in the number of ethnic marginals to 20 or 30
would not be politically important if governments
consistently enjoyed, for example, parliamentary
majorities of 100;

(d)   if the electoral gains the major parties achieved by
offering concessions to non-whites were not offset by
the loss of other critical votes. The potential electoral
benefits to the parties of courting non-whites would
probably have to exceed the expected electoral costs.[31]

These conditions probably could not be satisfied in the
foreseeable future. It is especially unlikely that all could be
satisfied simultaneously, as would be required in order for
ethnic marginals to give non-whites significant political
leverage. The strong attachment of ethnic-minority voters to
Labour has already been noted. It is currently inconceivable
that non-whites would defect *en masse* to the Conservatives or
other political parties. Equally inconceivable is that the
Conservative party successfully could or would shed its anti-
immigrant identity. Illiberal, racial sentiment too deeply
pervades the party at all levels.[32] It is also unlikely that ethnic
marginals could tip the political balance in the House of
Commons. Even if 25 ethnic marginals eventually emerged,

[29] To date, Conservative party managers and strategists have demonstrated much
more interest in detaching Asian than Afro-Caribbean voters from Labour.

[30] The Conservative party would have to be willing to 'outbid' Labour for the
support of ethnic-minority voters.

[31] The number of potential ethnic-marginal constituencies that could be won
would have to exceed the number of non-ethnic marginals that might be lost.

[32] Marian Fitzgerald, *Political Parties and Black People*, London, Runnymede Trust,
1984, pp. 20–1.

how politically important would they be, given the present Conservative hegemony in Parliament? Moreover, if the Conservatives' hegemony eroded after the next general election, as it might, would not the number of non-ethnic marginal constituencies probably also substantially rise, thus weakening the impact of an increase in the number of ethnic marginals?

With regard to the fourth condition—the net electoral gain the parties might achieve by offering tangible concessions to non-whites—Crewe has persuasively argued:

On the generous assumption that the ethnic minorities are fully registered, turn out to vote at the same rate as whites, and split 9 : 1 in Labour's favour, this ethnic increment has been worth a 1.1 per cent two-party swing to Labour. In 1979 that was equivalent to 12 seats *over 30 years*. It is hard to believe that the white anti-ethnic vote has been worth less to the Conservatives over the same period. At one election alone, in 1970, the national impact of Enoch Powell's speeches on immigration was almost certainly greater. Estimates vary, but of the three published the most cautious assesses their effect as a 1.5 per cent swing. Some of that effect will have stuck, and to it can be added the impact of the Conservative party's 'tough' stand on immigration in 1979. The concentration of ethnic electors in some marginal seats has almost certainly been outmatched by the spread of anti-ethnic electors across all marginal seats.[33]

It is especially unlikely that the Conservative party could maximize its total general-election vote *or* its marginal-seat victories by offering concessions to non-whites. Indeed, if either party courted the ethnic-minority vote too vigorously it would probably lose considerable white electoral support.

Are non-whites then without political influence? Is this diverse constituency condemned to exercising political voice through riots or other extra-parliamentary protest? Under conditions of political consensus between the major parties, such as prevailed for most of the 1960s and 1970s, one would have to be pessimistic about the prospects for the representation of non-white interests through conventional political channels. However, the recent erosion of the post-war inter-party consensus has visibly altered the political environment and, in the process, created within the Labour party an

[33] Crewe, 'Representation and Ethnic Minorities', p. 276.

opportunity for non-whites to gain a political voice which could not be achieved through electoral politics. In the new environment, ethnic minorities have joined a chorus of voices within the Labour party demanding and, to a degree, achieving political representation.[34] Non-white aspirations for institutional representation within the Labour party have focused most recently on the struggle for 'black sections'.

BLACK SECTIONS AND INTERNAL LABOUR POLITICS

The black-sections movement is a product of both Labour's past and Labour's present. It is a product of the past in that ethnic-minority demands for greater political representation within the party would never have coalesced had Labour's leaders not neglected this constituency and repeatedly sacrificed its interests on the altar of the racial consensus. It is a product of Labour's present in that a non-white pressure group initiative could not now garner significant activist support, let alone gain political influence, if the post-war consensus had not eroded and made Labour more penetrable from below. The black-sections initiative should thus be seen as a campaign by non-white Labour activists to exact retribution for the party's past neglect of their interests and to fabricate semi-permanent structures to prevent these interests from being neglected in the future. Perhaps more importantly, the current conflict over black sections within Labour highlights the advantages and limitations of a non-white strategy of representation through the party.

The black-sections movement advocates that non-white caucuses at the constituency, regional, and national tiers of the Labour party be formally established and that non-white party members be automatically included on the general management committees and executive committees of Labour's local parties and its National Executive Committee.[35] The movement has three essential aims:

---

[34] See e.g. Dennis Kavanagh, 'Representation in the Labour Party', in, Dennis Kavanagh (ed.), *The Politics of the Labour Party*, London, Allen and Unwin, 1982, pp. 202–22.

[35] Hugh Roberts, *Black Sections in the Labour Party*, London, Ernest Bevin Society, 1984, p. 2.

(a) recruitment/participation: to recruit non-whites into the Labour party and to encourage them to participate actively in the affairs of the party;

(b) accountability: to promote non-white party officials and the adoption of non-white political candidates within a structure which makes them accountable to Labour's non-white rank and file;

(c) representation: to pressure Labour leaders to include issues relevant to ethnic minorities on the party's national policy agenda.[36]

Unofficial non-white caucuses have operated in several Greater London parliamentary constituencies since 1980; by 1986 approximately 35 were in existence representing over 1,000 members. The first annual black-sections conference in Birmingham in 1984 attracted over 250 activists. However, the initial proposal to incorporate black sections into the Labour party's national structure was contained in a resolution moved by the Hendon South constituency party at the 1983 Annual Labour Conference. It petitioned the National Executive Committee to create a special panel which would:

(a) produce proposals for the necessary constitutional amendments . . . for ensuring greater involvement and more equal representation of disadvantaged groups at all levels of the party;

(b) give serious consideration to proposals for mandatory inclusion of members of disadvantaged groups on parliamentary shortlists wherever such members apply;

(c) recognize the right of black members of the party to organize together in the same way as Women's Sections and Young Socialist branches.[37]

The Hendon South motion was never put to a vote, but it prodded the NEC to create the Working Group on Positive Discrimination in February 1984 and, subsequently, the more permanent Black and Asian Advisory Committee.[38] However, non-white party activists have generally perceived these

[36] Ibid., pp. 5–13; and Socialist Action, *Black Sections Yes!*, London, Socialist Action Pamphlet, 1985, p. 10.

[37] As reproduced in, *Report of the Annual Conference of the Labour Party 1983*, London, Labour Party, 1983, p. 260.

[38] 'Black MPs Will Work As Caucus', *The Times*, 2 Oct. 1986, 4.

bodies as unrepresentative of the ethnic-minority community. As a consequence, a number of emotionally charged motions in favour of black sections have been forwarded to each of the last three Annual Labour Party Conferences. Most of the motions implicitly argue that non-whites have in the past been ignored or assimilated within the present structure and that Labour's leaders cannot be trusted, in the absence of formal, organized, and persistent political pressure, to advance ethnic-minority interests and adhere to a racially liberal course.

Paradoxically, disaffection from Labour among non-white activists coalesced at a juncture when the party appeared very receptive to progressive race policies. As Fitzgerald and Layton-Henry point out:

The growing importance of race issues for members of the Parliamentary Labour Party can be seen in the extremely large number of matters raised in the House by opposition MPs. These ranged from immigration controls and the 'sus' law to the treatment of Rastafarians in prison, the need for racially mixed juries and the use made of section 11 funds.[39]

Indeed, the contrast with the period of racial consensus, when race-related issues were infrequently raised and debated in Parliament, is considerable. Why, then, have non-white Labour activists rebelled during the 1980s and not before?

The black-sections movement and the political agitation of non-whites generally are primarily a function of and response to two converging trends: expanding opportunities for non-white political voice within the Labour party; and the increasing undesirability of Labour defection or 'exit'.[40] The first trend is closely linked to the continuing realignment of Labour's leadership and its receptivity in recent years to constituency parties and grass-roots interests which were neglected during the heyday of the post-war political consensus.[41] It is manifested in part by the increasing

---

[39] Marian Fitzgerald and Zig Layton-Henry, 'Opposition Parties and Race Policies, 1979–83', in, Z. Layton-Henry and P. B. Rich (eds.), *Race, Government and Politics in Britain*, London, Macmillan, 1986, p. 100.

[40] Hirschman, op. cit.

[41] Philip Williams, 'The Labour Party: The Rise of the Left', in, Hugh Berrington (ed.), *Change in British Politics*, London, Frank Cass, 1984, pp. 26–55.

numbers of local, non-white Labour councillors who have been elected since 1977 and the rise in the attendance of ethnic-minority activists at the Labour Party Annual Conference.[42] In sum, as non-whites have gained opportunities for voice and representation within the party, they have increasingly seized these opportunities. The undesirability of exit from Labour is a function of the Conservative party's current illiberalism on race-related issues. Political voice within the Labour party is the only course available to non-white activists who, by virtue of the two major parties' continued domination of British national politics and the indifference of the Social and Liberal Democratic party to ethnic minorities, have been denied an acceptable exit option.[43] Since non-whites have no shortage of legitimate grievances, it is logical that they should agitate for redress of these grievances through the Labour party.

Why should increased opportunities for and the efficacy of political participation through Labour precipitate the specific demand for black sections? The advocates of black sections hope to 'freeze' and extend what otherwise might prove to be an ephemeral opportunity for significant political representation. Through black sections non-whites intend to consolidate what modest, internal political leverage they currently enjoy. The black-sections movement operates on the assumption that the Labour party's recent ideological 'opening' to ethnic minorities will not necessarily endure. Just as the party initially elevated race-related issues to political prominence and then depoliticized them in the early 1960s so, many non-white activists believe, this pattern could be repeated in the 1980s. Such fears are not unfounded. As a prominent black-sections proponent, Russell Profitt, reminded Labour's Annual Conference in 1985:

We have been here before. Let us go back first to 1962—the first immigration control Act. Labour was at that time in a quandary. What should it be doing about the rights of the black communities in Britain? . . . What did the Labour party do? They set up a committee . . . under the Chair of no less a person than Harold Wilson. . . . This led to a statement called *Integrating the Immigrant*

---

[42] Crewe, 'Representation and Ethnic Minorities', pp. 277–8.
[43] Donley T. Studlar, ' "Waiting for the Catastrophe": Race and the Political Agenda in Britain', *Patterns of Prejudice*, 19.1, Jan. 1985, 7.

and, believe it or not, it suggested a liaison organization called the 'The British Overseas Socialist Fellowship'. . . . What did it do? Nothing, comrades.

Let us go back to 1964. We have memories, even if the leadership does not. There was a general election in the air at the time and Labour realized again that it had no policies on race, so another committee was set up. . . . What happened? It never completed its task. . . . In fact, it never said anything which has had an impact on the rights of black people . . . in this country.

Comrades, I have been on those committees. . . . Committees do not work. Black sections do. . . . Why? Because they are not patronizing talking shops. They are not about salving the consciences of middle-class do-gooders.[44]

Profitt's remarks reveal that the black-sections movement is explicitly conscious of the Labour party's historical vacillations on race and its negative implications for the future of non-white political representation.

The four outcomes or prospects for non-white political representation under conditions of racial consensus and competition can be represented schematically (see Table 7.5). Boxes one and three represent the options which were available to non-whites during the period of racial consensus (1964–75); with the disintegration of the consensus (1975–88), ethnic minorities confront choices two and four.

TABLE 7.5. *Non-white prospects for political representation*

	Consensus/ Depoliticization	Competition/ Politicization
Labour Voice	1. Partially Effective	2. Effective
Labour Exit	3. Mostly Ineffective	4. Ineffective

As Table 7.5 suggests, non-whites are especially disadvantaged politically during a period of inter-party consensus on race. Because of the indifference or, in some quarters of the party, the open hostility of Conservatives to ethnic-minority interests, exit from Labour is virtually excluded as an option.

[44] As reproduced in, *Report of the Annual Conference of the Labour Party 1985*, London, Labour Party, 1985, pp. 30–1.

Although voice within Labour is somewhat more effective than exit from Labour, it is only marginally so. When both party leaderships agree to exclude race-related issues from the political agenda, as occurred during the period of racial consensus, the efforts of non-whites to gain representation through Labour will not strike a responsive chord in the party as a whole. The ability of Labour's leaders to discipline or circumvent critics of the racial consensus within their own party will make it difficult for non-whites to find Labour allies to champion their interests. Moreover, ethnic minorities will not gain direct or easy access to Labour's key policy-makers, as access from the grass roots under conditions of political consensus is generally restricted to all but the most powerful interests. Whatever political advantages non-whites do receive will be delivered from above. Indeed, Labour's flawed anti-discrimination statutes were conceived and enacted with little input from non-whites.[45]

However, when party competition is renewed, the prospects for ethnic-minority interests to be politically represented improve. With Labour's rediscovery of its core socialist ideological identity, non-white interests, as well as those of other minorities in the party, are elevated. Ethnic minorities gain leverage and representation not because of their numerical strength, but because of the convergence of their struggle and the wider political objectives of the leadership, and particularly its interests in rejuvenating the party's grass roots and projecting a new, more 'radical' political image. Party leaders will especially respond to the grass roots when party morale is depressed after a period of protracted electoral failure. In these circumstances, Hirschman argues, voice forces

the party to trade its . . . vote-getting objectives to some extent against the discontent-reducing objective. Such a trade-off becomes even more likely when the inevitable uncertainty about prospective . . . votes is taken into account. In other words, a party which is beleaguered by protests from disgruntled members because they dislike proposed 'wishy-washy' platforms or policies will often be tempted to give in to these voices because they are very real here and

---

45 See Chris Mullard, *Black Britain*, London, Allen and Unwin, 1973, pp. 75–88.

now, while the benefits that are to accrue from wishy-washiness are highly conjectural.[46]

The good will and unity that leaders can obtain from the party by responding to the voice will impel them, at least in the short term, to sympathize with a wide range of minority demands. The recent receptiveness of Labour's leaders, and especially former racial Centrists like Roy Hattersley, to the unique interests of non-whites can partly be explained by their desire to revitalize the party following Labour's 1979 and 1983 election débâcles.[47]

LABOUR'S INTERNAL CONTRADICTIONS

Responding to ethnic-minority voice does not, however, necessarily mean that Labour party élites will acquiesce to non-white activist pressures for formal, institutional representation. Within the most democratic political party and under the most favourable of political conditions, grass-roots demands for greater representation would normally be received unenthusiastically by party leaders. Fearful of ceding even partial control over the course of party policy, party leaders automatically resist pressure by grass-roots interests to institutionalize their influence.[48] In accordance with this pattern, Labour's leaders have vehemently opposed black sections.

More than a dozen resolutions advocating black sections were forwarded by Labour's constituency parties and subsequently condensed by the Conference Arrangements Committee into composite motions before the 1984, 1985, 1986, and 1987 Annual Labour Party Conferences. Since Labour's National Executive Committee opposed these motions, each was defeated in general conference votes by overwhelming margins.[49] Since 1984 the NEC has offered three arguments

---

[46] Hirschman, op. cit., p. 70.

[47] Marian Fitzgerald, *Black People and Party Politics in Britain*, London, Runnymede Trust, 1987, pp. 30–1.

[48] Maurice Duverger, *Political Parties*, London, Methuen, 1978, pp. 133–5.

[49] Darcus Howe and Leila Hassan, 'Defeat for Black Sections', *Race Today*, 16.2, Dec. 1984, 8–10; and Richard Ford and Robert Morgan, 'Leaders Reject Black Section Backing', *The Times*, 3 Oct. 1987, 4.

against black sections: they could depress the political participation of non-whites in the party by segregating ethnic minorities from the larger Labour movement; they would reinforce already existing racial schisms within the working class; they would raise problems of racial definition and inclusion. Adopting a moral defence of the NEC's position, Labour's deputy leader Roy Hattersley argued in 1985:

> We believe black sections to be wrong . . . because . . . it is an article of socialist faith that all men and women be treated the same. We cannot insist that all men and women are treated the same . . . if then we choose to treat the races differently within the Labour party itself. Treating them differently would involve . . . breaches of . . . absolute principle.[50]

Replying on behalf of the NEC to a conference debate on black sections in 1987, Cyril Amber asserted:

> We seek integration, not separation and segregation. . . . [Black people] must play their role within the party and the constitution and not on their own terms.[51]

Other NEC representatives have demonstrated greater sympathy for black sections, but Labour's principal spokesmen on race-related policy, including the deputy leader, shadow Home Secretary, and the party leader Neil Kinnock have consistently been opposed to their adoption at the national level. The collective political weight of the opposition to black sections virtually ensures that they will not be incorporated soon into Labour's national, constitutional structure.

Although Labour's leaders have publicly resisted black sections on ethical and moral grounds, their opposition is more possibly motivated by broad, political considerations. Apart from the potential electoral damage the party could suffer if it is seen by the general electorate as too accommodating to non-whites—perhaps a minor risk given Labour's already close identification with ethnic-minority interests[52]—there are the more important requirements that party-élite

---

[50] *Report of the Annual Conference of the Labour Party 1985*, op. cit., p. 37.
[51] As cited in, *The Times*, 3 Oct. 1987.
[52] See Christopher T. Husbands, 'Race and Immigration', in Tony Atkinson *et al.*, *Socialism in a Cold Climate*, London, Allen and Unwin, 1983, pp. 161–83.

control over racial policy be maintained, and grass-roots pressures for intra-party 'democracy' be contained. Maintaining control over policy and containing democratic pressures are, of course, imperative for élites within all potential parties of government and not only Labour. As McKenzie argues:

Oligarchy in political parties helps to preserve for the leaders of a party (when they constitute the government) the necessary freedom of action, in the course of 'attending to the arrangements of society', to permit them to take into account all other group volitions and demands in that society.[53]

However, for Labour's leaders, managing the politics of support, including the support of its activists, and reconciling its requirements with those of the politics of governing have always been especially difficult. In particular,

the party's formal commitment to the proposition that the annual conference of the mass party determines party policy has led to perennial intra-party conflicts of a sort which have seriously undermined public confidence in the party and made the Labour party a less effective contender for power than would otherwise have been the case.[54]

As the adoption of formal black sections would significantly increase the influence of the annual conference and activists over national party policy it is predictable that Labour leaders would oppose them. On the other hand, given Labour's democratic ethos, which pervades the party at all levels and, among other things, celebrates the accountability of élites and grass-roots participation, it is hardly surprising that ethnic-minority activists would strongly resent being excluded from Labour's formal decision-making inner circles.[55]

Also disturbing to Labour's leaders is the possibility that demands for black sections could rekindle intra-party conflict on race, although probably along axes different from those which divided the party in the 1960s. Proponents of black sections have been fiercely criticized in recent years by the

[53] Robert McKenzie, 'Power in the Labour Party: The Issue of "Intra-Party Democracy" ', in, Dennis Kavanagh (ed.), op. cit., pp. 197–8.
[54] Ibid., pp. 199–200.
[55] See H. M. Drucker, *Doctrine and Ethos in the Labour Party*, London, Allen and Unwin, 1979.

left-wing faction, Militant, and prominent figures on Labour's ideological right.[56] In itself, such conflict could be managed but, following on the heels of Labour's 1983 and 1987 general-election defeats and the party's internecine squabbles over defence issues, an interminable row over black sections could jeopardize the precarious party unity so carefully cultivated by the post–1983 Kinnock leadership. Concern for party unity very much pervaded the reply of the deputy leader Roy Hattersley to the 1985 Conference debate on black sections:

I have no doubt that . . . debate [on black sections] will continue and the National Executive has no wish to suppress it. But it must be conducted in . . . a way that enhances rather than damages the prospects of the Labour party.

The only way of replacing the racist immigration regulations is a Labour Government. The only way of repealing the British Nationality Act and replacing it with an instrument which discriminates neither against the blacks nor the Asians nor women is a Labour Government. . . . Anyone who conducts this debate in a way which damages the prospects of a Labour Government damages the black and Asian British more than they damage anybody else.[57]

The anxieties of Labour's leaders about disharmony and its potentially negative effects on Labour's electoral fortunes are understandable. As Labour's racial Centrists of the 1960s were well aware, a conflict-ridden Labour party *is* penalized by the electorate and is probably more vulnerable politically than an equally or more divided Conservative party.[58]

SOCIAL AND LIBERAL DEMOCRATS: A VIABLE ALTERNATIVE
TO LABOUR?

Up to this point we have focused on the Labour party as the 'natural' political representative of non-whites and we have argued that Labour is more ideologically committed than the

---

[56] Socialist Action, op. cit.; 'Black Votes: Mixed Blessing', *The Economist*, 18 Apr. 1987, pp. 58–9; and 'Party Conjurer Sent to Work Blacks' Magic', *Observer*, 3 May 1987.

[57] *Report of the Annual Conference of the Labour Party 1985*, op. cit., pp. 38–9.

[58] McKenzie, op. cit., pp. 199–200; and *The Economist*, 14 Mar. 1987, p. 55.

Conservative party to ethnic-minority interests. Yet, as Studlar has correctly observed, the 'Liberals have consistently been the most favourable toward racial minorities of the three traditional parties' and the 'Liberal/SDP Alliance more likely to pose the greatest challenge to Labour domination of black support'.[59] During the period of racial consensus when the Conservative and Labour parties were becoming increasingly illiberal on race, the Liberal party opposed legislative initiatives to restrict Commonwealth immigration and consistently supported anti-discrimination statutes.[60] Is, then, the new Social and Liberal Democratic party a viable and attractive political alternative to Labour? Would ethnic-minority interests perhaps be better represented by the Democratic party when and if it becomes a credible alternative party of government?

While projections of the future political behaviour of the SLD are, at best, speculative, there are reasons to suspect that, if it found itself in government, the party would probably represent ethnic-minority interests less aggressively than Labour. This tentative conclusion follows from several factors. First, the SLD would be politically cross-pressured on race. Like the major parties, which each split into several factions in the 1960s and 1970s, a more tightly organized SLD would likely divide in the future between racially progressive, former Liberals and activists of the less racially liberal, old SDP. Divisions between the two Alliance partners on race, Fitzgerald argues, are already evident and are likely to increase once the SLD approaches power:

Like any other party, the Alliance will be tempted to balance its desire for black support against its need to retain and extend its white support to the maximum. It will also encompass a range of attitudes towards the question of racial equality, some of which fall short of its official image. Some of the resultant tensions appear already as between the two Alliance parties themselves. Thus [before the 1983 general election] the Liberals compromised their ... commitment to repeal the Nationality Act and reached agreement with the SDP that the Alliance would simply be

    [59] Studlar, 1985, op. cit., 6.
    [60] See Stan Taylor, 'The Liberal Party and Immigration Control: A Study in Policy Deviance', *New Community*, 8.1, Spring–Summer 1980, 107–14.

committed to 'amending' the Act. There was resentment also among some Liberals that they were not able to follow up recommendations they had made after the riots of 1981.[61]

Divisions within the Alliance on race were also evident in 1983 when Liberal parliamentary candidates were much closer to Labour than SDP candidates in their opinion of the 1971 Immigration Act and somewhat closer to Labour candidates in their attitude toward the 1981 British Nationality Act (see Table 7.6). The ideological constraints and/or cross-cutting

TABLE 7.6. *Parliamentary-candidate opinion on recent race legislation, 1983 (% of candidates polled)*

	Support	Support with improvements	Disapprove	Don't know
Immigration Act (1971)				
Labour	2	15	77	6
Liberal	–	25	62	14
SDP	5	64	17	14
Race Relations Act (1976)				
Labour	22	70	5	3
Liberal	12	74	9	5
SDP	21	70	2	8
Nationality Act (1981)				
Labour	1	1	95	4
Liberal	–	6	92	2
SDP	–	14	80	6

Source: Muhammad Anwar, *Ethnic Minorities and the 1983 General Election*, London, CRE, 1984.

pressures which inhibited the advancement of ethnic-minority interests by the major parties during the racial consensus, therefore, are not unique to nor a consequence of two-partism and remain relevant for the Social and Liberal Democrats in the late 1980s. Only if and when these are reconciled will the SLD emerge as an alternative vehicle for the advancement of the political interests of non-whites.

[61] Fitzgerald, 1984, op. cit.

Second, as the political heir of the Butskellite legacy, the Original Social Democratic party up to 1987 had been averse to policies which could polarize the electorate or undermine its carefully cultivated centrist image.[62] Despite its highly publicized 'radical' pretensions, the SDP remained committed to the essential pillars and political *modus operandi* associated with the post-war political consensus. As with Harold Wilson's Labour party of the 1960s, the SLD's aversion to political 'hot potatoes' is only likely to increase the closer the party moves toward government and its race policies are scrutinized more carefully by a still predominantly illiberal electorate. On this score Labour would appear to be a safer political choice than the Alliance for non-whites. A socialist Labour party is more ideologically committed to the poor, the disadvantaged, and the politically unorganized in British society. Moreover, as the party which is currently supported by two-thirds or more of ethnic-minority voters, it already has some electoral incentive to pursue policies beneficial to non-whites. Indeed, several analysts have implied that Labour's commitment to ethnic-minority interests is likely to strengthen if, as has occurred recently, the non-white vote increases as a percentage of Labour's total electoral support.[63] Although the Labour party's response to ethnic-minority interests in Ealing does not necessarily support this thesis, the relationship between ethnic minorities and the Labour party has probably been reinforced to the advantage of non-whites over time by the political dominance of Labour in areas where non-white voters are residentially concentrated.[64]

Moreover, in generally speculating about the proclivity of small third parties of government (a status to which the Social and Liberal Democratic party aspires) to be responsive we perhaps need look no further than West Germany. Despite genuine multipartism in that country, the main German

---

[62] See Ian Bradley, *Breaking the Mould*, Oxford, Martin Robertson, 1981, pp. 120–38. To the degree that the old SDP did move away from Butskellism, especially in economic affairs, it gravitated toward the more populist positions of the Conservative party.

[63] Fitzgerald, 1984, op. cit., p. 31; and Studlar, 1985, op. cit., p. 5.

[64] In 1986 11 of 14 London boroughs with a non-white population of over 15 per cent were Labour-controlled. Labour also controlled 33 of 51 parliamentary seats in constituencies with the highest ethnic-minority population.

political parties, including the liberal Free Democratic party, do not respond to grass-roots interests much better than their British counterparts. Serious problems of citizen and interest 'exclusion' in West German politics persist.[65] For the most part, a political dynamic is at work in West Germany which was visible until fairly recently in British politics. Whenever elections regularly produce close results (in terms of the numerical balance of parliamentary seats) all potential parties of government, including the smallest, are motivated to avoid issues and interests which threaten their parliamentary seat maximization strategy, *regardless of their traditional ideological orientation or previous manifesto commitments.* As we saw in Chapter 4, it is primarily the drive and realistic opportunity for political office in highly electorally competitive circumstances which motivate potential parties of government to ignore small and potentially divisive, cross-cutting interests. Hence, one could reasonably expect that when and if the SLD moves closer to government, given its weaker ideological commitment to ethnic minorities and its disposition toward centrist policies, it would probably be less responsive to non-white interests than a more ideologically motivated Labour party.

ETHNIC-MINORITY POLITICIANS

Much scholarly and media attention has focused recently on the rising number of ethnic-minority candidates contesting and gaining political office.[66] Impressive progress has been achieved recently on this front: for example, 27 non-white parliamentary candidates represented Britain's three main parties in the 1987 general election, in contrast to 18 in 1983, only 5 in 1979, and 2 in 1974. In 1987 4 of 14 non-white Labour parliamentary candidates were elected to the House of

---

[65] See e.g. the conflict in West Germany over nuclear power in Dorothy Nelkin and Michael Pollak, *The Atom Besieged*, Cambridge, Mass. MIT Press, 1982. Approximately 30% of the electorate in 1981 believed that an environmentalist party was needed in West Germany. David P. Conradt, *The German Polity*, New York, Longman, 1981, p. 128.

[66] See e.g. Susan Welch and Donley T. Studlar, 'Voting for Minority Candidates in Local British and American Elections', paper presented at the Conference on Ethnic and Racial Minorities in Advanced Industrial Democracies, Univ. of Notre Dame, 3–5 Dec. 1987.

Commons (see Table 7.7), all of whom support the general campaign for black sections. Several Labour insiders as late as July 1985 had predicted that the party was on course to select

TABLE 7.7 *Successful ethnic-minority parliamentary candidates, 1987*

Candidate	Constituency	Labour Majority (%)	Swing from 1983 (%)	Turnout (%)
B. Grant	Tottenham	8.2	(L. to C.) 6.8	66.1
K. Vaz	Leicester E.	3.7	(C. to L.) 2.8	78.6
P. Boateng	Brent S.	19.5	(L. to C.) 3.4	64.9
D. Abbott	Hackney N.	19.8	(L. to C.) 1.8	58.1

Source: *The Times*, 13 June 1987.

between 20 and 25 ethnic-minority parliamentary candidates.[67] On the local level, the number of non-white councillors in London boroughs rose from 35 in 1978 to 79 in 1984 to over 130 after the May 1986 local elections. Birmingham has 14 non-white local councillors, and the Labour group in the Council in the London borough of Brent is led by a black woman.

The election of an increasing, albeit still disproportionately small, number of non-whites to political office obviously constitutes progress in the integration of ethnic minorities into the mainstream of British political life. Without the elevation of non-whites to all levels of government, it is difficult to envisage how ethnic-minority interests can gain a secure place on the national and local public-policy agendas. However, if the recent experience of electing black and Hispanic mayors in American cities offers any comparative lessons, they are that the unique interests of the ethnic minorities in Britain will not necessarily be represented well by elevating ethnic-minority politicians to high political office.[68] The election of greater numbers from the ethnic minorities to Parliament and even to local councils in Britain is probably a necessary but not a sufficient condition to produce concrete policies favourable to non-whites.

[67] Mark Crail, 'Labour on Target for 25 Black Candidates', *Tribune*, 19 July 1985.
[68] See e.g. Carlos Muñoz Jr. and Charles Henry, 'Rainbow Coalitions in Four Big Cities: San Antonio, Denver, Chicago, and Philadelphia', *PS*, 19.3, Summer 1986, 598–609.

Indeed, given the prominent role of political parties as vehicles of interest representation and policy formulation in British politics, the election of greater numbers of ethnic-minority politicians will probably have less impact on the course of public policy than would be the case in the United States where these traditional party functions were ceded to other institutions some time ago and where individual politicians have greater opportunities to shape the political agenda. A tradition of strong political parties coupled with unitary and parliamentary government in Britain virtually requires that non-whites first become influential within the major political parties in order to effect meaningful policy change. The elevation of non-white issues on the political agenda in London through the now defunct Greater London Council is a recent instance of the successful penetration of sub-national government by individual ethnic minorities.[69] However, in most localities, elected non-white representatives must co-operate with white Labour leaders and other party activists in order to realize specific policy objectives. Moreover, in an environment where the autonomy of local government is being incrementally eroded, where since the mid-1970s the political, legal, and financial authority of local government have been undermined by central government,[70] the election of greater numbers of non-white local councillors in the future will have less impact politically than it would have had previously. In Britain the power to effect policy change still primarily flows through the major political parties and, increasingly, it is power which is meaningfully exercised only at the level of national politics.

There is every indication that black-sections activists appreciate the continuing relevance of party to achieving policies outcomes favourable to ethnic minorities in Britain. Unlike many contemporary feminists, nuclear disarmers, environmentalists, and other 'natural' left-wing constituencies who have recently adopted extra-party vehicles, the black-sections movement has attempted to capture a fragment of the

[69] See Fitzgerald, 1987, pp. 30–1.

[70] Mike Goldsmith and Ken Newton, 'Central–Local Government Relations: The Irresistible Rise of Centralized Power', in, Hugh Berrington (ed.), op. cit., pp. 216–33.

Labour party in order to promote its agenda in the national, political arena. Regardless of the immediate prospects for the success of this initiative, two points must be conceded in its favour: (*a*) given the persistence of racial illiberalism in Britain, the receptiveness of current Labour-party leaders to non-white concerns, and the illiberal proclivity of the Conservative party, the initiative for black sections is a *rational* strategy to advance the interests of non-whites at the national level; and (*b*) black sections are a potentially effective vehicle for advancing ethnic-minority concerns over time and regardless of change in the climate of opinion both within the Labour party and the larger political environment. Given the recent electoral setbacks the Labour party has suffered, a strategy for black sections is unlikely to yield tangible results in the short term. However, it would appear to be the most direct and politically secure route to meaningful ethnic-minority influence in national politics in the future.

CONCLUSIONS

The campaign for black sections will, of course, have to be endorsed by a broader constituency than Labour's most militant non-white activists in order to be ultimately effective. More immediately, the proponents of black sections will have to garner the support of a significant segment of non-white Labour voters before the party's leaders will reconsider their opposition. On both fronts political change appears to be moving in favour of black sections. The little survey evidence which existed before 1987 indicated that only a small minority of the ethnic-minority electorate supported the campaign for black sections; according to a 1984 Harris survey only 16 per cent of the ethnic-minority community in London—where activist agitation for black sections has been most intense—approved of separate race sections within the major parties.[71] However, more recent evidence indicates that the black-sections campaign is now endorsed by a third of all ethnic-minority voters nationwide (see Table 7.8). Of particular

[71] Peter Kellner, 'David Blunkett is Right about Sharon Atkin', *New Statesman*, 17 Apr. 1987.

TABLE 7.8. *Non-white attitudes on Labour black sections, 1987*
(% of respondents)

	Total	Voting Intentions			Ethnic Group	
		Conser-vative	Labour	Alliance	Asian	Afro-Caribbean
Approve	33	25	39	22	31	39
Disapprove	45	57	44	58	46	44
Don't know/						
Not stated	21	18	17	20	23	17

Source: *Harris Research Survey*, 25–9 May 1987, Richmond, Harris Research Centre.

relevance to the eventual fate of the campaign is the finding that Asians are about as enthusiastic as Afro-Caribbeans about black sections and that support for black sections rises to 39 per cent among non-whites who intended to vote Labour in the 1987 general election. This level of support is probably still too small to persuade Labour's leaders to adopt black sections. However, it is a sizeable popular base on which the black-sections campaign might build additional support.

8

Conclusions

The absence of race from party–political discussion in Britain between 1964 and 1975, after its emergence as a salient political issue, signalled the suspension of party competition in this area of public policy. For more than a decade, Conservative and Labour leaders attempted to extricate race from electoral politics by excluding race-related issues from inter-party debate and election manifestos; enacting cosmetic anti-discrimination statutes in conjunction with increasingly restrictive immigration rules; and financially supporting local and national racial buffers. While removing race from the official political agenda, however, these strategies did not significantly diminish the salience of race within the British electorate. On the contrary, by avoiding problems of race relations and non-white immigration, the major parties further politicized this area of public policy by deflecting the conflict and public debate over race into political channels outside party politics.

Indeed, as we saw in Chapters 2 and 5, party efforts to depoliticize race were ineffective in allaying public concerns. Throughout the 1960s and early 1970s, public opinion polls revealed that a substantial percentage of voters felt that too many immigrants had been admitted into Britain and that immigration constituted one of the most urgent problems confronting the country; even into the 1980s, more than 80 per cent of the electorate thought that controlling immigration was very important and, despite the passage of a series of restrictive immigration measures by successive governments, almost half of all voters felt that the political parties were not addressing themselves to the immigration issue adequately. As we saw in Chapter 5, thousands of citizens expressed their disillusionment with the parties and their consensus on race by supporting the opponents of consensus. Enoch Powell's sudden rise to national political prominence and the enormous popularity he enjoyed in the late 1960s and early 1970s were direct products of his repudiation of the racial consensus. The growth of extra-parliamentary movements opposed to the silence of the parties on racial problems also reflected public dissatisfaction with the parties. Unlike the major political parties, the National Front and the Anti-Nazi League gave political voice to popular sentiments on race. As long as the Conservative and Labour parties continued to neglect race-related issues, these extra-parliamentary groups flourished.

Buffeted by the pressures of anti-consensus spokesmen and party-linked pressure groups clamouring for change, the Conservative party, and then Labour, disengaged from the racial consensus. Since the mid–1970s race-related subjects have become more frequent topics of intra-party discussion; inter-party differences on race have visibly widened; and the race policies of the post–1979 Conservative governments have been challenged by the Opposition. As in the earlier period of 'fundamental debate' on race (see Chapter 2), each major party has recently adopted coherent racial policies which are not automatically endorsed by its political opponent. Moreover, the renewal of party competition on race has reinforced the Conservative party's anti-immigrant proclivity and Labour's ideological identification with the interests of non-whites.

The disengagement of the Conservative party from the racial consensus and its adoption of an explicit illiberal posture on race after 1975 were facilitated by the election of Margaret Thatcher as party leader. Apart from her instinctive distrust of consensus politics, Thatcher brought to Conservative-party race policy a personal set of illiberal opinions. For Labour, the liberal orientation of its National Executive Committee and the Labour Party Race Action Group pressured the party to repudiate much of its past legislative record and adopt progressive race policies. For both parties the racial consensus had become less important as the political conditions under which it had been forged in the 1960s had altered. In particular, the disappearance of the Conservative party's colonial-paternalistic wing and Labour's apparently growing stake in securing the ethnic-minority vote influenced each party to reformulate its race policies.

The impetus to extricate race from party politics can be traced to the sharp intra-party schisms which race engendered after 1958 and the persistence of illiberal public attitudes on the subject. The intensification of these divisions in the early 1960s threatened to undermine political party unity and alienate that critical fraction of the electorate, the so-called floating voters, whom Conservative and Labour leaders believed decided British elections. These voters were perceived as important because of the relatively small vote swing at British general elections in the 1950s and 1960s and the near-equal representation of the parties in Parliament. Operating on the assumption that floating voters were political 'moderates', Conservative and Labour leaders deliberately avoided issues which might jeopardize their centrist political strategy. The absence of an obvious centre posture on race suggested that the subject could only be politically neutralized if it were withdrawn from the electoral market-place by both major parties.

The strategy to depoliticize race and other divisive issues assumed that electoral parity would persist into the indefinite future, and appealing to floating voters produced greater electoral returns than satisfying traditional supporters. As Gamble describes Conservative thinking on immigration after the party was defeated in the 1966 general election:

There was talk of the need to retrench, but Heath had decided . . . that 'appealing to those who did not vote for us was more important than simply appeasing those who did'. . . . It was the middle ground, the floating vote, that was always what was most important. The shift to the right on immigration and crime threatened the [party's] appeal to the centre.[1]

By the late 1970s both assumptions had been undermined by political events. In particular, the haemorrhaging of partisan and electoral support for both major parties, and Labour's increasing inability to obtain a working majority in the House of Commons threw the parties back on to core constituencies

---

[1] Andrew Gamble, *The Conservative Nation*, London, Routledge, 1974, p. 101.

opposed to policy consensus. In the shift toward competitive party politics, race again became a subject of inter-party conflict.

Had race been an exceptional issue which the major parties only temporarily neglected, then their 'responsiveness' after 1975 might be seen as belated but inevitable. It could be argued that party competition on race, although considerably delayed, was not deliberately suspended. However, this perspective does not explain the active strategies that the major-party leaders pursued to depoliticize race-related issues. Moreover, it ignores the wider political context in which the race policies of the Conservative and Labour parties were conceived and implemented. As we argued in Chapter 1, race was not atypical but, rather, one of a number of issues which the parties depoliticized, and their consensus to depoliticize these issues part of a broader pattern of collusive party behaviour which prevailed for much of the post-war era. Defended and promoted by a generation of Conservative and Labour leaders, the parties' post-war political consensus fostered party competition on subjects of marginal importance and party convergence on many salient public-policy issues, including economic and political management issues central to the governance of Britain.

CONSENSUS WITHOUT CONSENT

The convergence of the Conservative and Labour parties' policies in government, the similarity of their campaign appeals and themes, and their tacit understanding to exclude a number of salient issues from the political agenda raise doubts about the practical benefits to the electorate of intense two-party electoral competition. Notwithstanding the relative closeness of their electoral support and parliamentary representation—indeed perhaps because of these—the major parties' contest for office restricted the range of policy options offered to voters and, in many areas of public policy, inter-party debate did not occur. Contrary to Downsian expectations, the Conservative and Labour parties' electoral competitiveness did not make them responsive to the concerns of voters.[2] The tendency of Britain's post-war party system to under-represent or inadequately represent non-élite interests raises the pertinent question of how it was possible for the major parties to neglect salient, race-related issues?

The bipartisan consensus to keep race off the political agenda, as we saw in Chapter 2, was facilitated by the highly centralized, hierarchical, and élite-dominated nature of the major parties. The relative unaccountability of party leaders to party members and their rank-and-file activists and the domination of the major parties by their political 'centre' allowed an inter-party policy agreement to be forged and, once forged, to endure. Generally, the pliability of the constituency associations of the parties during the Butskellite period virtually guaranteed that an élite-initiated policy consensus on race be respected by party sub-leaders at the national and local levels.[3] As we saw in Chapter 6, the considerable success Conservative and Labour leaders enjoyed in defusing party conflict on race did not mean that intra- and inter-party policy differences were resolved; rather, party leaders did not allow, especially during election periods, these conflicts to surface publicly. Through a mixture of political coercion, persuasion, and manipulation, Conservative and Labour leaders preserved party discipline on race for more than a decade. Dissenting party sub-leaders who openly challenged the racial consensus were likely to be dealt with severely, as Enoch Powell discovered when he was expelled in 1968 from the Conservative shadow cabinet.

Also facilitating the efforts of the major parties in keeping race off the political agenda were the difficulties anti-consensus groups and spokesmen experienced in articulating their views through mainstream political channels. Perhaps the chief structural obstacles to political voice and influence for opponents of the racial consensus were: (*a*) Britain's single-member, relative-majority electoral system; and (*b*) a disciplined, two-party system.

Britain's first-past-the-post electoral system penalized opponents of the racial consensus: first, by raising a for-

[2] Albert O. Hirschman, *Exit, Voice, and Loyalty*, Cambridge, Mass., Harvard Univ. Press, 1970, p. 3.
[3] R. T. McKenzie, *British Political Parties*, London, Praeger, 1963.

midable structural barrier to the formation of a national ethnic-minority, or exclusively race-oriented, protest party;[4] and second, when such a party did coalesce and contest general elections, as in the case of the National Front, by denying it parliamentary representation.[5] The lack of a parliamentary foothold primarily deprived the anti-consensus forces of a regular and highly visible platform from which to expose and exploit the inadequacies of the Conservative and Labour parties on race. In so doing, it drove these forces into extra-parliamentary channels which were not only less politically influential than parliamentary ones but also viewed by the electorate more suspiciously and as less legitimate.[6] One need only compare the strategic advantage of protest parties represented in the French National Assembly and the West German Bundestag, for instance, to appreciate how much more vulnerable the racial consensus would have been to external challenge, had the National Front and/or the party equivalent of the Anti-Nazi League gained parliamentary representation in Britain.[7] Particularly in West Germany, the Green party has effectively used its parliamentary platform in the 1980s to attack the policy consensus of the major parties on nuclear power and other environmental issues.[8]

The chief effect of Britain's disciplined two-party system was to inhibit opponents (liberal or illiberal) of the racial consensus within the parties from traversing party boundaries and initiating a co-operative campaign to undermine the consensus. Tribal, partisan loyalties, ideological prejudices, and fear of antagonizing pro-consensus party leaders

[4] Ivor Crewe, 'Representation and the Ethnic Minorities in Britain', in, Nathan Glazer and Ken Young (eds.), *Ethnic Pluralism and Public Policy*, London, Heinemann, 1983, pp. 260–1.

[5] Under a system of pure proportional representation, for example, the National Front would have gained 4 parliamentary seats as a result of the May 1979 general election. Ivor Crewe, 'The Voting Surveyed' in *The Times Guide to the House of Commons May 1979*, London, Times Books, 1979, p. 253.

[6] The illegitimacy of the ANL's anti-Front Campaign was often the theme of media accounts. See e.g. Hugo Young, 'Peter Hain and the Forces of Darkness', *Sunday Times*, 17 Sept. 1978.

[7] The French National Front, for example, has been fairly successful at publicizing its illiberal racial views. See Daniel Cohen, 'Trouble on the Right', *Atlantic*, Feb. 1985, 26–34; and *The Economist*, 5 Jan. 1987, 46.

[8] See e.g. Joyce M. Mushaben, 'The Changing Structure and Function of Party: The Case of the West German Left', *Polity*, 18.3, Spring 1986, 431–56.

restrained intra-party, anti-consensus factions from building bridges to like-minded counterparts in the political opposition.[9] The reluctance of Conservative dissidents to work with Labour activists and, particularly, Enoch Powell's unwillingness to join forces with race pressure groups (like the National Front and the Monday Club) isolated the critics of consensus, diluted their political influence, and put them at a competitive disadvantage *vis-à-vis* consensus proponents who, especially in Parliament, successfully transcended their partisan differences.[10] Dissidents on race were not, of course, uniquely disadvantaged. Intra-party critics of the major parties' consensus on the EEC in the 1970s were also reluctant to unify and, hence, equally ineffective in combating the bipartisan, pro-EEC juggernaut.[11] On both race and the EEC the anti-consensus critics closely reflected majority public sentiment. However, the informal and formal constraints of two-party politics inhibited the opponents of consensus from capitalizing politically on the considerable public sympathy for their positions.

RACE, PARTY COMPETITION, AND THE POLITICAL AGENDA

Whatever their previous handicaps, anti-consensus forces within the parties are currently ascendant. In 1988 the Conservative and Labour parties are as diametrically opposed on race issues as has been the case at any point during the past two decades. Unlike their counterparts of the early 1960s, neither major-party leadership has a compelling or immediate interest in allowing policy differences on race between the parties to narrow. Moreover, intra-party discussion on race-related issues is no longer overtly suppressed, especially within Labour. In short, party competition on race, as on several other salient subjects previously avoided by the major parties during the Butskellite era, has been renewed.

---

[9] Racially liberal Conservative activists, e.g. did not join their Labour counterparts in supporting the Anti-Nazi League.

[10] See Ch. 2.

[11] See David Butler and Uwe Kitzinger, *The 1975 Referendum*, London, Macmillan, 1976.

What does the renewal of party competition presage for the future of race in British politics? As long as party-competitive conditions prevail, race will be a relevant topic of intra- and inter-party discussion, but such discussion is only the first step in the formation of responsive public policy. Unfortunately for the electorate, party competition will not solve Britain's racial dilemmas. In itself, party competition on race will not lead inevitably to the further restriction of non-white immigration, reduce racial violence and physical attacks on ethnic minorities, eliminate racial discrimination and disadvantage, promote harmonious race relations, or foster peace between the police and black youth in Britain's decaying inner cities. Party competition will not effect, as has been vividly demonstrated by events associated with the 1981 and 1985 riots, a dramatic improvement in the urban environment in which many non-whites reside.[12]

Party competition will not inevitably produce these results because it is concerned with the articulation and representation of popular interests. Party competition is not a process for 'solving' economic, political, and social problems. Through party competition the public agenda and the policy agendas of the political élite substantially converge, and the central concerns of the electorate are accurately represented in public, political debate and the electoral arena. How well parties act upon citizen concerns in government is not directly relevant to party competition because problem-solving success depends on many variables exogenous to parties.[13] On the other hand, parties choose the issues they discuss or ignore and the interests and constituencies they represent. It is on the basis of these decisions that political parties compete for the support of the electorate.

Moreover, party competition does not ensure that race will gain a permanent place on Britain's national political agenda. The renewal of party competition will not determine the future status of race in British politics primarily because party

[12] For a summary of the events associated with the 1981 and 1985 riots see Ceri Peach, 'A Geographical Perspective on the 1981 Urban Riots in England', *Ethnic and Racial Studies*, 9.3, July 1986, 396–411; John Benyon (ed.) *Scarman and After*, Oxford, Pergamon, 1984; and Zig Layton-Henry, 'Immigration and Race Relations: Political Aspects No. 14', *New Community*, 13.1, Spring–Summer 1986, 119–25.

[13] Richard Rose, *Do Parties Make a Difference?*, London, Macmillan, 1980.

competition will elevate race-related issues on Britain's political agenda only so long as these issues are salient to a substantial number of voters.[14] In this regard, several observers have commented that race has become less important in recent years. Specifically, it has been argued that the virtual termination since 1981 of non-white immigration into Britain has diminished the public's interest in race-related questions. While race is undoubtedly less politically salient in the late 1980s than it was at the height of the bipartisan consensus, it has hardly become peripheral to British political affairs. Many issues seemingly unrelated to race, in which the electorate is intensely and unambiguously interested, have a racial dimension. An obvious public policy area historically linked with race, for example, is 'law and order'. Indeed, the Conservative party has explicitly suggested and reinforced this linkage in the 1980s.[15] Second, the salience of race, as with most public policy issues, naturally fluctuates over time. Given that race-related conflict persists, the salience of race has probably only temporarily diminished. This area of public policy will remain potentially explosive in Britain into the indefinite future. Thus, race is likely to be included on the national political agenda as long as party competitive circumstances prevail.

Although party competition will not necessarily resolve Britain's racial problems, it will aid political élites in identifying and ranking these difficulties and, in doing so, facilitate solutions. Indeed, perhaps the worst product of the Conservative and Labour parties' consensus on race was élite neglect of race-related problems which, over time, grew worse. As we saw in Chapters 2–5, the efforts by the major parties to depoliticize race produced no panacea. Between 1964 and 1975 racial intolerance did not significantly abate, Community Relations Councils failed to integrate ethnic minorities into the mainstream of British life, racial disadvantage at the local level persisted, and a window of opportunity was opened

---

[14] It is appropriate to add that the electorate expresses its sentiments most effectively through strong parties. See Walter D. Burnham, *Critical Elections and the Mainspring of American Politics*, New York, Norton, 1970.

[15] Marian Fitzgerald, *Black People and Party Politics in Britain*, London, Runnymede Trust, 1987, p. 49.

for the emergence and growth of violent, racial-hate groups like the National Front, thus exacerbating racial tensions. The suspension of party competition had the effect of postponing the public political discussion vital to informing sober and representative élite policy decisions. As we saw in Chapters 6 and 7, the renewal of party competition has already initiated the necessary, if somewhat turbulent, public political dialogue on race.

POLITICAL EXPRESSION AND REPRESENTATION THROUGH POLITICAL PARTIES

Throughout this book we have focused on the response of the Conservative and Labour parties to Britain's post–1958 race-related difficulties. We specifically examined the racial consensus of the major parties and the motivations and factors behind its formulation and disintegration. Guiding our analysis have been three implicit assumptions which we now wish to elaborate and make explicit: (*a*) since the 1950s the political parties have been at the centre of Britain's racial difficulties; (*b*) the Conservative and Labour parties' response to race-related issues have almost exclusively shaped the post–1958 politics of race; (*c*) political parties are the only effective vehicle of popular political expression and representation on race-related issues.

If there is a common perception which has informed virtually all British post–1958 scholarship on race, including this study, it is that political parties have consistently been at the centre of race-related conflict. Although scholars sharply disagree about where to assign blame for Britain's racial problems, few deny the centrality of parties in the evolution and resolution of these difficulties.[16] This simple truth is pregnant with implications. Apart from the fact that it justifies the title and central focus of this book, the historical responsibility parties bear for Britain's racial problems has inextricably linked the credibility of, if not popular support

---

[16] For a criticism of the parties see Michael Dummett and Ann Dummett, 'The Role of Government in Britain's Racial Crisis', in Lewis Donnelly (ed.), *Justice First*, London, Sheed and Ward, 1969, pp. 25–79.

for, parties to the state of British race relations.[17] This historical role has undermined attempts by the parties themselves to devolve responsibility for racial problems to apolitical, buffer institutions, and it has politicized race-related public policy.

The close association of the parties with racial conflict in the public mind has undoubtedly motivated citizens to express their race-related concerns politically. Whether one considers the initiatives of the Anti-Nazi League, National Front, or pressure groups such as the Monday Club, Labour Party Race Action Group, and the recently organized black-sections movement, all of these were unambiguously political.[18] This fact should not be taken for granted. The early emergence of Community Relations Councils and other apolitical race bodies might have influenced citizens to perceive race as a social issue to be appropriately dealt with by national and local social-welfare bodies. There is little intrinsic to race-related conflict which a priori suggests the primacy of political solutions. However, given that the parties were responsible for allowing, if not encouraging, non-white immigration and were generally perceived as responsible by the British public, opponents of a multiracial society and racial liberals alike generally perceived the parties not as incompetent firemen, unable to contain the blaze of racial conflict, but as arsonists. As Sarlvik and Crewe discovered in their analysis of electoral opinion after the 1979 general election: 'The British public would prefer that the [race] question had never arisen; that is, the prevailing feeling was that the country should not have let in so many immigrants in the first place.'[19] Indeed, race is probably one of only a few salient public-policy issues during the post-war period for which the electorate held the parties almost exclusively

[17] See Daniel Lawrence, 'Race, Elections, and Politics', in, Ivor Crewe (ed.), *British Political Sociology Yearbook, vol. 2: The Politics of Race*, London, Croom Helm, 1975, p. 62.

[18] The British churches, for example, were not as centrally involved in Britain's racial conflict as they were in the early anti-nuclear movement of the 1950s and 1960s nor were they as politically active as the Christian churches were in the American South during the US civil-rights movement.

[19] Bö Sarlvik and Ivor Crewe, *Decade of Dealignment*, CUP, 1983, p. 242.

responsible.[20] As a result, race could not be easily de-politicized.

To speak of party responsibility for racial conflict is, of course, to include only the Conservative and Labour parties. As the hegemonic actors in post-war British politics, the leaders of the major parties set the tone and defined the parameters of public, political debate on race-related issues. Few British voters, for instance, were aware of, let alone influenced by, the Liberal party's progressive racial platform.[21] The National Front and the Anti-Nazi League were primarily reactive groups, which responded to the policies and positions adopted by the major parties. Neither the NF nor the ANL shaped public racial opinion as well as they articulated it; neither movement could influence public racial attitudes as effectively as a timely speech by Hugh Gaitskell, Enoch Powell, or Margaret Thatcher.[22] Most importantly, only the major parties, as a consequence of their duopoly over national political power, could implement racial policy at the national level.

The ultimate consequence of the major parties' responsibility for and dominance of the post–1958 politics of race was that once party competition on race was suspended, race-related issues disappeared from the political agenda. In the absence of party competition, a succession of close general elections and regular party rotation in office in the 1960s and 1970s did not alter the peripheral status of race in British

[20] A. M. Messina, 'Toward an Alternative Explanation for British Party Decay', unpublished paper, 1986. The EEC is another issue on which the parties were vulnerable to criticism.

[21] Stan Taylor, 'The Liberal Party and Immigration Control: A Study in Policy Deviance', *New Community*, 8.1–2, Spring–Summer 1980, 112–13.

[22] In a curious piece of logic Studlar argues that anti-immigrant sentiment has historically been so strong in Britain that 'élite political initiatives, either pro- or anti-immigration, could be of only limited influence. When there is a staunch 60 per cent majority under any circumstances wanting further immigration restrictions, there is little room for élite actors to influence public opinion.' Donley T. Studlar, 'British Public Opinion, Colour Issues, and Enoch Powell: A Longitudinal Analysis', *British Journal of Political Science*, 4.3, July 1974, 376. Yet, his own data indicate that the Labour party's opposition to non-white immigration restrictions in 1961 influenced 14% of the electorate to alter their attitudes on the subject in only a one-month period. What would have been Labour's influence if the party had consistently and visibly maintained its opposition to immigration controls over the period of a decade?

government. Under conditions of two-partism and disciplined parliamentary government, the postures on race adopted by the Liberals or extra-parliamentary race groups were largely irrelevant to the electorate. Although open, competitive elections ultimately held governments accountable for their policies, the diversity of public opinion and interests on race-related issues were not adequately reflected in the national, political agenda.

This reality highlights the significance of party-competitive politics as a process for articulating and channelling non-élite political demands and interests. More significantly, however, it underscores the crucial importance of responsive and representative political parties to democratic politics. The problem of oligarchy in political parties, and specifically post-war British parties of government, has not been a central concern of this study.[23] Nevertheless, after surveying the post–1958 politics of race, it is difficult not to conclude that oligarchy in the Conservative and Labour parties was a serious impediment to meaningful party competition on race-related issues and, hence, to the representation of citizens' interests. In this connection it is perhaps pertinent to recall Hirschman's remarks on political party responsiveness:

The best possible arrangement for the development of party responsiveness to the feelings of members may . . . be a system of just a few parties, whose distance from each other is wide, but not unbridgeable. In this situation, exit remains possible, but the decision to exit will not be taken lightheartedly. Hence voice will be a frequent reaction to discontent with the way things are going and members will fight to make their voice effective.[24]

Over the past decade or so it has been fashionable in scholarly circles to lament the breakup of the post-war political consensus and the polarization of British party politics.[25] These developments, it has been argued, are detrimental to

[23] This was, of course, a central preoccupation of R. Michels, *Political Parties*, New York, Collier, 1962.
[24] Hirschman, op. cit., p. 84.
[25] See e.g. S. E. Finer, *The Changing British Party System 1945–79*, Washington, D.C., American Enterprise Institute, 1980; and Stephen Haseler, *The Tragedy of Labour*, Oxford, Basil Blackwell, 1980.

the best interests of the British electorate. Maybe so. However, if the story of the Conservative and Labour parties' consensus on race offers any lessons, it is that the convergence of party policies and élite political consensus without popular consent are not without cost. The cost to political parties may or may not be diminished electoral support. The cost to the nation is certainly the fallout which results from neglected public problems.

Select Bibliography

Benyon, J. (ed.), *Scarman and After*, Oxford, Pergamon, 1984.
Downs, A., *An Economic Theory of Democracy*, New York, Harper and Row, 1957.
Fitzgerald, M., *Political Parties and Black People*, London, Runnymede Trust, 1984.
Foot, P., *Immigration and Race in British Politics*, Harmondsworth, Penguin, 1965.
——— *The Rise of Enoch Powell*, Harmondsworth, Penguin, 1969.
Freeman, G. P., *Immigrant Labor and Racial Conflict in Industrial Societies*, Princeton, Princeton University Press, 1979.
———*The Conservative Nation*, London, Routledge, 1974.
Gamble, A. M., *The Conservative Nation*, London, Routledge, 1974.
Economic Policy 1945–83, London, OUP, 1984.
Glazer, N., and Young, K. (eds.), *Ethnic Pluralism and Public Policy*, London, Heinemann, 1983.
Hill, M. J., and Issacharoff, R. M., *Community Action and Race Relations*, London, OUP, 1971.
Hirschman, A. O., *Exit, Voice, and Loyalty*, Cambridge, Mass., Harvard University Press, 1970.
Husbands, C. T., *Racial Exclusionism and the City*, London, Allen and Unwin, 1983.
Jacobs, B. D., *Black Politics and Urban Crisis in Britain*, London, CUP, 1986.
Katznelson, I., *Black Men, White Cities*, London, OUP, 1973.
Layton-Henry, Z., *The Politics of Race in Britain*, London, Allen and Unwin, 1984.
Layton-Henry, Z., and Rich, P. B. (eds.), *Race, Government and Politics in Britain*, London, Macmillan, 1986.
Miles, R., and Phizacklea, A. (eds.), *Racism and Political Action in Britain*, London, Routledge, 1979.
Mullard, C., *Black Britain*, London, Allen and Unwin, 1973.
Newton, K., *Second City Politics*, London, OUP, 1976.
Robertson, D., *A Theory of Party Competition*, London, Wiley, 1976.
Rose, E. J. B., and Associates, *Colour and Citizenship*, London, IRR/OUP, 1969.

Schoen, D. E., *Enoch Powell and the Powellites*, New York, St. Martin's, 1977.

Schumpeter, J. A., *Capitalism, Socialism, and Democracy*, New York, Harper and Row, 1976.

Taylor, S., *The National Front in English Politics*, London, Macmillan, 1982.

Walker, M., *The National Front*, Glasgow, Fontana, 1978.

Index

Index compiled by Peva Keane